KEEP THIS MAJOR WORK
UP TO DATE

It is the intention of LLP Limited to keep all major works up to date and ensure that our customers have the very latest information.

A supplement to this work is planned and we would like to ensure that you receive this as soon as it is published. To reserve your copy, simply return this card. You may also use it to order additional copies of *Enforcement of Maritime Claims, 2nd edition.*

Please reserve for me .... copies of the forthcoming supplement to *Enforcement of Maritime Claims, 2nd edition.* I understand that you will send me a pre-payment invoice prior to publication.

Please send me .... additional copies of *Enforcement of Maritime Claims, 2nd edition* (ISBN 1 85044 302 5) at £125 each.

Other available titles
Please send me details of: (tick box)
Lloyd's Shipping Law Library ☐
Lloyd's Commercial Law Library ☐

Please send me a copy of your complete catalogue ☐

|L|L|P|

Method of Payment
☐ Payment enclosed (payable to LLP Limited) in £ Sterling.
☐ Please send me a pre-payment invoice. (Goods will be despatched on payment of invoice.)
☐ Please debit my credit/charge card:

☐ Amex ☐ Diners ☐ Visa ☐ Access/Mastercard

Card No.: ☐☐☐☐☐☐☐☐☐☐☐☐☐☐☐☐

Signature: .... Expiry Date: .... / ....

Note: When paying by credit card please quote registered card address.

If you are in an EC Country please provide the VAT registration number of your company: ....

Postage and packing charges
UK: Please add £5 per book
Overseas: Please add £10 for one book, £15 for two or more books.

Please give your preferred delivery address:

Name (Mr/Mrs/Miss): ....

Job Title: ....

Company Name: ....

Address: ....

....

Town/City: .... Postcode: ....

Country: ....

Tel: ....

Orders from North America and the Far East will be processed by our relevant overseas offices in local currency.

KEEP THIS MAJOR WORK
UP TO DATE

It is the intention of LLP Limited to keep all major works up to date and ensure that our customers have the very latest information.

A supplement to this work is planned and we would like to ensure that you receive this as soon as it is published. To reserve your copy, simply return this card. You may also use it to order additional copies of *Enforcement of Maritime Claims, 2nd edition.*

Please reserve for me .... copies of the forthcoming supplement to *Enforcement of Maritime Claims, 2nd edition.* I understand that you will send me a pre-payment invoice prior to publication.

Please send me .... additional copies of *Enforcement of Maritime Claims, 2nd edition* (ISBN 1 85044 302 5) at £125 each.

Other available titles
Please send me details of: (tick box)
Lloyd's Shipping Law Library ☐
Lloyd's Commercial Law Library ☐

Please send me a copy of your complete catalogue ☐

|L|L|P|

Method of Payment
☐ Payment enclosed (payable to LLP Limited) in £ Sterling.
☐ Please send me a pre-payment invoice. (Goods will be despatched on payment of invoice.)
☐ Please debit my credit/charge card:

☐ Amex ☐ Diners ☐ Visa ☐ Access/Mastercard

Card No.: ☐☐☐☐☐☐☐☐☐☐☐☐☐☐☐☐

Signature: .... Expiry Date: .... / ....

Note: When paying by credit card please quote registered card address.

If you are in an EC Country please provide the VAT registration number of your company: ....

Postage and packing charges
UK: Please add £5 per book
Overseas: Please add £10 for one book, £15 for two or more books.

Please give your preferred delivery address:

Name (Mr/Mrs/Miss): ....

Job Title: ....

Company Name: ....

Address: ....

....

Town/City: .... Postcode: ....

Country: ....

Tel: ....

Orders from North America and the Far East will be processed by our relevant overseas offices in local currency.

CUSTOMER SERVICES
BOOK ORDER DEPARTMENT
LLP LIMITED
FREEPOST
SHEEPEN PLACE
COLCHESTER
ESSEX CO3 4BR
ENGLAND

CUSTOMER SERVICES
BOOK ORDER DEPARTMENT
LLP LIMITED
FREEPOST
SHEEPEN PLACE
COLCHESTER
ESSEX CO3 4BR
ENGLAND

ENFORCEMENT OF MARITIME CLAIMS

SECOND EDITION

LLOYD'S SHIPPING LAW LIBRARY

Laytime and Demurrage
second edition
by John Schofield
(1990)

The Ratification of Maritime Conventions
edited by The Institute of Maritime
Law, University of Southampton
(1990)

Admiralty Jurisdiction and Practice
by Nigel Meeson
(1993)

*Contracts for the Carriage of Goods
by Land, Sea and Air*
by David Yates *et al.*
(1993)

Marine Environment Law
by John H. Bates and Charles Benson
(1993)

Voyage Charters
by Julian Cooke,
Timothy Young, Andrew Taylor
John D. Kimball, David Martowski
and LeRoy Lambert
(1993)

EC Shipping Law
first edition
by Vincent Power
(1992)
first supplement
(1994)

Enforcement of Maritime Claims
second edition
by D. C. Jackson
(1996)

Marine War Risks
second edition
by Michael D. Miller
(1994)

Merchant Shipping Legislation
by Aengus R. M. Fogarty
(1994)

*CMR: Contracts for the International
Carriage of Goods by Road*
second edition
by Andrew Messent
with David Glass
(1995)

Multimodal Transport
by Ralph De Wit
(1995)

Ship Sale and Purchase
second edition
by Iain S. Goldrein *et al.*
(1993)
first supplement
(1995)

Time Charters
fourth edition
by Michael Wilford, Terence Coghlin
and John D. Kimball
(1995)

The Law of Shipbuilding Contracts
second edition
by Simon Curtis
(1996)

The Law of Tug and Tow
by Simon Rainey
(1996)

ENFORCEMENT OF MARITIME CLAIMS

SECOND EDITION

BY

D. C. JACKSON
Professor of Law at the
University of Southamption

LONDON   NEW YORK   HONG KONG
1996

LLP Limited
Legal & Business Publishing Division
27 Swinton Street
London WC1X 9NW

USA AND CANADA
LLP Inc.
Suite 308, 611 Broadway
New York, NY 10012, USA

SOUTH EAST ASIA
LLP Asia Limited
Room 1101, Hollywood Centre
233 Hollywood Road
Hong Kong

© D. C. Jackson, 1996

First edition, 1985
Second edition, 1996

British Library Cataloguing in Publication Data
A catalogue record
for this book is available
from the British Library

ISBN 1–85044–302–5

Text set 10 on 12 pt Times by
Interactive Sciences, Gloucester
Printed in Great Britain by
Hartnolls Ltd, Bodmin, Cornwall

Preface

This work is an examination of issues relevant to the enforcement of maritime claims in an English court. With the addition of a chapter on limitation of liability it updates and builds on the first edition and also covers the area of *Civil Jurisdiction and Judgments —Maritime Claims* (1987). Of particular and developing significance is the effect of European Conventions on jurisdiction and recognition of judgments and the law governing contractual matters. As a result of these Conventions the general structures relating to jurisdiction and judgments are different according to whether the matter falls within or outside an applicable Convention.

The book is in five parts.
    Part I encompasses:
        (1) the extent to which a connection is required between England and a dispute for an English court to hear and determine the dispute;
        (2) the characteristics of the actions *in personam* and *in rem* as methods of enforcing a claim;
        (3) restrictions on the exercise of the powers of an English court to hear and determine a dispute;
        (4) time restrictions on the bringing and pursuit of a claim;
        (5) the availability and nature of arbitration as an alternative to litigation.
    Part II is a discussion of interim relief and the extent to which, if at all, a claimant can ensure that the defendant's assets are available to satisfy a judgment.
    Part III is concerned with the security interests in assets—particularly those created as a consequence of making a claim through an action *in rem*. There is a detailed examination of the concept of a lien, the connections between a lien and the action *in rem*, the characteristics of different types of lien and priorities between liens. Finally in this part, a short chapter is devoted to the complex question of the creation of liens by contract, particularly in charterparties and bills of lading.
    Part IV deals with the question at the heart of the pursuit of any claim—the remedy available and likely to be awarded and limitations there may be on the amount of damages.
    Part V is concerned with the foreign element more often than not part of a maritime claim—the law which governs particular issues before an English court and the recognition or enforcement of foreign judgments.
    Relevant legislative and Convention texts are set out in the appendices.

I am grateful to the publishers for their aid and encouragement, to my colleagues of the Institute of Maritime Law and the Faculty of Law for their valued advice and assistance, to my secretary Mrs Marion Dalton for her continued expertise in deciphering illegible manuscript and her unlimited patience throughout drafts, and to my wife for the countless aspects of support that she gives.

DAVID JACKSON

Outline Table of Contents

Preface   v
Table of Cases   xli
Table of Statutes   lxvii
Table of Statutory Instruments   lxxix
Table of Conventions   lxxxiii

INTRODUCTION. MARITIME CLAIMS AND THEIR
    CONSEQUENCES   1

PART I. JURISDICTION AND MODES OF
    ENFORCEABILITY

Chapter 1   Sources of Admiralty jurisdiction   9
Chapter 2   The nature of maritime claims   19

PART II. JURISDICTION OF ENGLISH COURTS AND
    ARBITRAL TRIBUNALS

Chapter 3   Jurisdiction bases for enforcement of maritime claims   77
Chapter 4   The Brussels Convention—boundaries and structure   87
Chapter 5   The Brussels Convention—forum law or Convention regime?   101
Chapter 6   The Brussels Convention—jurisdiction allocation in initial
            proceedings   123
Chapter 7   Jurisdiction as between England, Scotland and Northern Ireland   159
Chapter 8   The Lugano Convention—divergence from the Brussels
            Convention   169
Chapter 9   Enforcement of maritime claims by an action "in personam" 171
Chapter 10 Enforcement of maritime claims by an action "in rem"   193
Chapter 11 Delay in suit   213
Chapter 12 Restrictions on jurisdiction   231
Chapter 13 Arbitration   273

PART III. INTERIM RELIEF

Chapter 14 Nature and basis of interim relief   295
Chapter 15 Arrest and alternative security   311
Chapter 16 The "Mareva" injunction   347

PART IV. SECURITY ON THE MERITS—THE LIEN CONCEPT

Chapter 17 Nature and development of liens   369
Chapter 18 Maritime liens   387
Chapter 19 Statutory liens in Admiralty   427
Chapter 20 Possessory liens   439
Chapter 21 Equitable liens   455
Chapter 22 Creating a lien by contract   461
Chapter 23 Priorities   471

PART V. REMEDIES

Chapter 24 Limitation of liability   515
Chapter 25 Remedies in actions on the merits   547

PART VI. FOREIGN LAW

Chapter 26 Application of foreign law   561
Chapter 27 Enforcement of foreign judgments and arbitral awards outside
            the Brussels and Lugano Conventions   607
Chapter 28 Judgments and settlements within the Brussels or Lugano
            Convention   625

APPENDICES

Appendix 1 Statutes   653
Appendix 2 Rules of the Supreme Court   729
Appendix 3 Conventions   749
Appendix 4 Private International Law (Miscellaneous Provisions) Act 1995,
            Parts III, IV   763

Index   767

Detailed Table of Contents

Preface	v
Table of Cases	xli
Table of Statutes	lxvii
Table of Statutory Instruments	lxxix
Table of Conventions	lxxxiii

INTRODUCTION. MARITIME CLAIMS AND THEIR CONSEQUENCES

1. The tripartite nature of maritime claims	1
The concept of "lien"—and its connection with arrest and jurisdiction	2
2. The relevance of a foreign element	2
3. Statutory and Convention development	3
Statutes	3
Until 1956	3
The Administration of Justice Act 1956	3
The Supreme Court Act 1981	4
Conventions enacted into English law	4
Civil Jurisdiction and Judgments Acts 1982 and 1991	4
4. Matching Statute and Convention	4

PART I. JURISDICTION AND MODES OF ENFORCEABILITY

CHAPTER 1. SOURCES OF ADMIRALTY JURISDICTION | 9

1. The Admiralty framework of the Supreme Court Act 1981	9
(i) The list of claims (s.20)	10
(ii) The "maritime lien" (s.21(3))	10
(iii) Actions "in personam" and actions "in rem" (s.21)	10
"Action in personam"	11
The Supreme Court Act 1981	11
"Action in rem"	11
The Supreme Court Act 1981	11
2. Sources outside the Supreme Court Act 1981	12
Admiralty, common law and equity	12
Common law and equity	12
Equitable intervention in the common law	13
The effect of registration requirements	13

Admiralty   14
Statutes, judicial creativity and Admiralty   14
Statutes enacting Conventions   15
   The EC Jurisdiction and Judgments Convention 1968 (as amended) (the
      Brussels Convention)   16
   The EC and EFTA Jurisdiction and Judgments Convention 1988 (the Lugano
      Convention)   16
The Civil Jurisdiction and Judgments Acts 1982 and 1991 and maritime claims   16

3. Conclusion   17

CHAPTER 2. THE NATURE OF MARITIME CLAIMS   19

1. Heads of jurisdiction—the framework of the Supreme Court Act 1981   19
Section 20(1)(a), (2)(4)(5)(6)   19
Section 20(1)(b), (3)   19
Section 21(3)   20
Section 20(1)(c)   20
Section 20(1)(d)   20

2. Application of the framework despite foreign connections (s.20(7))   20
Jurisdiction   20
The applicable law   20

3. Jurisdiction based on the past and the future   21
A. Looking to the past   21
   The "sweeping up" clause—"any other jurisdiction which it had immediately before
      the commencement of this Act" (s.20(1)(c))   21
   Jurisdiction conferred specifically by the Act of 1956—"damage received
      by a ship" (s.20(2)(e))   21
   The sweeping up provision of the Administration of Justice Act 1956 22
     Jurisdiction conferred by statute   22
     Non-statutory jurisdiction ("that was vested" prior to 1 November 1875) 22
     Construction of heads of claim in Supreme Court Act 1981 22
     Jurisdiction not referred to in Supreme Court Act 1981   22
B. Looking to the future   23
   Jurisdiction assigned to the Admiralty Court by Rules of Court (s.20(1)(d)) 23

4. Categories of enforceability   23
Claims enforceable by action "in rem"   24
   Effect of establishing a limitation fund   24
   (i) Claims attracting maritime lien or "other charge"   24
     (a) Uncertainties of maritime liens   25
     (b) Foreign maritime liens   26
     (c) Maritime liens and extension of jurisdiction by statute 26
     (d) Established maritime liens   26
     (e) Statutory extensions by analogy   42
     (f) Claims in respect of which a maritime lien has been suggested 43
     (g) "Or other charge"   45
   (ii) Claims enforceable by action in rem against the relevant property or ownership
      of a share in a ship   45
     (a) Claim to ownership or possession of a ship or share in a ship (s.20(2)(a)) 45

(b) Any questions arising between co-owners of a ship as to possession, employment
     or earnings of the ship (s.20(2)(b), 20(4))   46
(c) Any claim in respect of a mortgage of or charge on a ship or any share
     therein (s.20(2)(c), 20(7)(c))   47
(d) Any claims for the forfeiture or condemnation of ship or goods, the restoration
     of ship or goods after seizure or droits of Admiralty (s.20(2)(s))   48
(iii) Claims enforceable "in rem" against a ship or "sister ship" (s.20(2)(d)–(r))
     Jurisdiction and enforceability "in rem" compared   50
(a) Any claim for damage received by a ship (s.20(2)(d))   50
(b) Any claim for damage done by a ship (s.20(2)(e))   52
(c) Any claim for loss of life or personal injury, etc. (s.20(2)(f))   55
(d) Any claim for loss of or damage to goods carried in a ship (s.20(2)(g)) 56
(e) Any claim arising out of an agreement relating to the carriage of goods in a
     ship or to the use or hire of a ship (s.20(2)(h))   58
(f) Salvage (s.20(2)(j))   64
(g) Any claim in the nature of towage in respect of a ship (s.20(2)(k))   66
(h) Any claim in the nature of pilotage in respect of a ship (s.20(2)(l))   67
(i) Any claim in respect of goods or materials supplied to a ship for her operation
     or maintenance (s.20(2)(m))   67
(j) Any claim in respect of the construction, repair or equipment of a ship or in
     respect of dock charges or dues (s.20(2)(n))   69
(k) Any claim by a master or a member of the crew of a British or non-British ship
     for wages (including any sum allotted out of wages or adjudged by a
     superintendent to be due by wages) (ss.20(2)(o), and 24(2)(a))   69
(l) Any claim by a master, shipper, charterer or agent in respect of disbursements
     made on account of a ship (s.20(2)(p))   71
(m) Any claim arising out of an act which is or is claimed to be a general
     average act (s.20(2)(q))   71
(n) Any claim arising out of bottomry (s.20(2)(r))   72
Claims enforceable by action "in personam"   72
  Availability of action "in personam"   72
  Claims enforceable only by action "in personam"   73
  The categories of claim   73
(a) Any claim for damage received by a ship   73
(b) Any application in the High Court under the Merchant Shipping Act 1995
     (s.20(1)(b) and 20(3)(a))   73
(c) "Collision" actions (s.20(1)(b) and 20(3)(b))   73
(d) Limitation actions (s.20(1)(b) and 20(3)(c))   74
(e) The sweeping up clause (s.20(1)(c))   74

PART II. JURISDICTION OF ENGLISH COURTS AND ARBITRAL TRIBUNALS

CHAPTER 3. JURISDICTION BASES FOR ENFORCEMENT OF MARITIME CLAIMS   77

The substantive "jurisdiction base"   77
Service of process and jurisdiction bases   77
The development of jurisdiction bases   77
  Limitations on "writ" jurisdiction   77
  Convention jurisdiction requirements   78
  Enactment or incorporation of Conventions into English law   78

Types of Convention with jurisdiction provision   79

Particular jurisdiction bases   79
1. Convention text directly enacted   79
   (i) The Athens Convention 1974 (Merchant Shipping Act 1979, Sch. 3)   79
   (ii) The CMR 1956 (Carriage of Goods By Road Act 1965, Sch.)   80
   (iii) The Hague-Visby Rules 1968   81
2. Conventions reflected in English law   81
   (i) The Arrest Convention 1952   82
   (ii) The Collision (Civil Jurisdiction) Convention 1952   82
   (iii) The Oil Pollution Convention 1969 (to become the 1992 Convention on
        enactment of the 1992 Protocol on 30 May 1996)   83
   (iv) The Fund Convention 1971 (to become the 1992 Convention on enactment of
        the 1992 Protocol)   84
   (v) The Rhine Navigation Convention 1868 (as amended)   84
3. Conventions in force to which the United Kingdom is not a party   84

Generally applicable jurisdiction bases   85
The European Jurisdiction Conventions   85
The Brussels Convention 1968 (as amended)   85
The Lugano Convention   85
The influence of the Brussels and Lugano Conventions   86

CHAPTER 4. THE BRUSSELS CONVENTION—BOUNDARIES AND
    STRUCTURE   87

I. The General Pattern   87
Jurisdiction and judgments   87
Connections with the Community   87
Interpretation of the Convention   88
The role of national laws   88
Relationship with other Conventions   89
Application within the United Kingdom   89
Application to other United Kingdom territories   90

II. Applicability of the Convention   90
1. The subject-matter—"civil or commercial matters"   90
   The general definition   90
   The specific exclusions   91
     Bankruptcy   91
     Arbitration   92
         (i) The validity of an arbitration agreement   92
         (ii) Recognition of a judgment on the validity of an arbitration agreement   93
         (iii) Recognition of judgment in breach of arbitration agreement   93
         (iv) Consideration of the three aspects   93
2. Proceedings to which the Convention applies   94
   Proceedings falling outside the Convention   94
      (i) Cases having no foreign element   94
      (ii) Proceedings without a defendant   94
      (iii) "Multiple proceedings" as between courts of contracting and non-contracting
           States   95
      (iv) Proceedings to enforce judgments of non-contracting States   95
   Type of proceedings within the Convention   95

III. Consideration of Convention jurisdiction by adjudicating court 96
1. Declining jurisdiction 97
  "Of the court's own motion" 97
    "Of its own motion"—the obligation 97
  Other duties to decline jurisdiction 98
  The power to decline jurisdiction 98
2. Stay of proceedings 98
  Procedural safeguards as jurisdictional prerequisites 99

CHAPTER 5. THE BRUSSELS CONVENTION—FORUM LAW OR
  CONVENTION REGIME? 101

The basic dichotomy 101
Convention regime or national law? 101

Applicability of national law of the forum 101
A. Where defendant is not domiciled in a contracting State 101
B. Extension of scope of national law rules (Articles 2, 4) 102
C. Limitation actions 103

Applicability of the Convention regime 103
  1. Reference to another Convention—Article 57 103
  2. Brussels Convention jurisdiction bases 103
1. Criteria of applicability other than the defendant's domicile 103
  A. Exclusive jurisdiction by virtue of Article 16 104
    Matters within Article 16 104
      (i) Immovable property (Article 16.1) 104
      (ii) Corporations and associations (Article 16.2) 105
        The seat of the corporation 106
      (iii) Public registers (Article 16.3) 106
      (iv) Intellectual property (Article 16.4) 106
      (v) Judgments (Article 16.5) 107
  B. Appearance by a defendant (Article 18) 107
    "Appearance" in English law 108
  C. Jurisdiction by agreement (Article 17) 108
    "Exclusive" jurisdiction 110
    The formal requirements 111
      Oral agreement followed by writing 112
    Scope of Article 17 112
      (i) International disputes 112
      (ii) Set off 113
      (iii) Selection of more than one court 113
      (iv) Selection of court of a non-contracting State 113
    Waiver of the agreement 114
    Article 17 and third parties to jurisdiction agreements 114
    Article 17 and its limitations 115
      (i) Exclusive jurisdiction under Article 16 115
      (ii) Individual employment contracts 115
      (iii) An agreement for the benefit of one party 115
      (iv) Jurisdiction through "appearance" under Article 18 116
    Jurisdiction agreements in relation to insurance and consumer contracts 116
    Persons domiciled in Luxembourg 116
  D. Insurance and consumer contract regimes—"deemed domicile" 117

E. Limitation of liability (Article 6a)—the court hearing the liability action   117
2. The domicile of the defendant in a contracting State   118
    The concept of domicile   118
    Domicile of individual   118
        The general criteria of domicile of individuals   119
            Domicile in the United Kingdom   119
            Domicile in a state other than a contracting state   119
        Domicile of corporations and associations   119
            Domicile for the purposes of "exclusive" jurisdiction in company proceedings   120
        Domicile of trusts—section 45   120
        Domicile of the Crown—section 46   121
        Summary   121

CHAPTER 6. THE BRUSSELS CONVENTION—JURISDICTION
    ALLOCATION IN INITIAL PROCEEDINGS   123

1. Reference to another Convention (Article 57)   123
The scope and effect of the reference   123
    (i) Conventions overridden   124
    (ii) Conventions maintained   124
Relevant maritime law Conventions   125
    1. The Arrest Convention 1952   127
    2. The Collision (Civil Jurisdiction) Convention 1952   128
    3. The Oil Pollution Conventions 1969 and 1971   129
    4. Conventions concerning nuclear material and ships   130
    5. Conventions concerning carriage of goods by sea   131
        (i) The Hague Rules 1924 and Hague-Visby Rules 1968   131
        (ii) The Hamburg Rules 1978   131
        (iii) The Multimodal Convention 1980   132
        (iv) The CMR—Carriage of Goods by Road   132
        (v) The Athens Convention on Passengers and Their Luggage 1974   133
        (vi) The Limitation of Liability Convention 1976   134
        (vii) The Liens and Mortgages Conventions 1926, 1967 and 1993   135
        (viii) The Rhine Navigation Convention 1868   135

2. Mandatory allocation of jurisdiction   136

3. Optional allocation of jurisdiction   136
    (i) Claims for limitation of liability   137
    (ii) Pre-Convention written choice of law of Ireland or part of the United Kingdom   137
    (iii) Where the defendant is domiciled in a contracting State   138
        The primary principle   138
        The concept of domicile   138
    (a) Defendant domiciled in more than one contracting State   138
    (b) Special subject matter regimes—insurance and consumer contracts   139
    Insurance (section 3)   139
        Claim by insured   140
        Claim by insurer   140
        The jurisdiction agreement   141
            Marine risks covered by Article 12a   142
            Relationship between Articles 12 and 17   142

Consumer contract jurisdiction   143
  Jurisdiction agreements   144
(c) Options based on connecting factor other than domicile between contracting
    State and dispute   144
(1) Substantive claims   146
    (i) Contract (Article 5(1))   146
    Maritime wage disputes   146
    Persons domiciled in Luxembourg   147
    Ambit of Article 5(1)   147
        (i) "In matters relating to contract"   147
        (ii) "The place of performance of the obligation in question"   148
        "The obligation in question"   148
            Contracts of employment   149
        The place of performance   149
            Agreement by the parties to the place of performance   151
    (ii) Claims in tort or delict (Article 5(3))   151
        "Matters relating to tort, delict or quasi delict"   151
        "Place where the harmful event occurred"   151
        Place of the damage   152
        Evaluation of "harm"   152
    (iii) Remuneration for salvage (Article 5(7))   152
(2) Operations of a branch, agency or other establishment (Article 5(5))   153
    "Branch agency or other establishment"—a Community concept   153
        External evidence of the existence of the branch   154
        Connection between dispute and parent body   154
(3) Suing defendant in capacity as settlor, trustee or beneficiary of a trust
        (Article 5(6))   155
(4) Linked proceedings   155
    Limitation of liability (Article 6a)   155
    Civil claims in criminal proceedings (Article 5(4))   155
(d) Multi parties or actions   155
    Other Convention jurisdiction   156
    Co-defendants (Article 6(1))   156
    Third parties (Article 6(2))   157
    Counterclaims (Article 6(3))   158
    Contracts connected with rights "in rem" immovables (Article 6(4))   158

CHAPTER 7. JURISDICTION AS BETWEEN ENGLAND, SCOTLAND
    AND NORTHERN IRELAND   159

(a) Convention allocation to a place in the United Kingdom   159

(b) Domestic allocation following Convention allocation to the United Kingdom
    as a whole   160
Domicile of trust, consumer, supplier or insurer   160

(c) The intra United Kingdom structure   161
    The scheme is domestic   162
    The role of rules of court   162
Applicability of the adapted framework   162
    Subject-matter—"civil and commercial matters"   162
    Matters within the adapted framework   162
    Matters excluded   163
    Connecting links with the United Kingdom   163

The general pattern of the regime   163
Particular jurisdiction bases   164
    Primary basis of domicile of defendant in a part (Articles 2 to 4)   164
    "Exceptional category" cases (Articles 16, 17, 18)   164
        Mandatory criteria   164
            Exclusive jurisdiction (Article 16)   164
            Appearance (Article 18)   165
            Jurisdiction agreements (Article 17)   165
        Domicile and optional alternatives   165
            Specific subject-matter jurisdiction (insurance and consumer contracts) 165
            Plaintiff's options instead of defendant's domicile   165
                General alternatives (Articles 5 to 6a)   165
                    Link with dispute   165
                    Multi parties and multi claims   166
                    Limitation of liability   166
                Jurisdiction agreements (Article 17)   166
                    Jurisdiction agreement in consumer contracts   167
Procedural safeguards   167

CHAPTER 8. THE LUGANO CONVENTION—DIVERGENCE FROM
    THE BRUSSELS CONVENTION   169

Jurisdiction in maritime claims (Article 54A)   169

Individual employment contracts   169
 (i) Jurisdiction agreements (Article 17)   169
(ii) Place of performance (Article 5(1))   170

Relationship to Brussels Convention (Article 54B)   170

CHAPTER 9. ENFORCEMENT OF MARITIME CLAIMS BY AN ACTION
    "IN PERSONAM"   171

The claims for which an action "in personam" is available   171

Nature of the action "in personam" as compared to the action "in rem"   171

Jurisdiction in actions "in personam"   172
Jurisdiction through service of a writ   173
The writ "in personam"   173
    Amendment of a writ   175

Service in England   175
    Individuals   175
    Corporations   176
Steps following service   176
Through an action "in rem"   177
    Bail   178

Service of a writ outside England   179
RSC Order 11 (for text see Appendix 2)   179
    Service without leave   179

The Civil Jurisdiction and Judgments Act 1982 (the Brussels Convention) 180
Service with leave 180
Categories of claim for serving out 182
RSC Order 11 183
Seeking an injunction 184
The merits 185
The appropriate forum 185
Service of the writ (with or without leave) 186
(i) Service by the plaintiff or his agent 187
Relevance of foreign law 187
(ii) Service through governmental, judicial or consular authority 187
RSC Order 75 188
The categories of claims and the discretion to permit service out 188
Oil pollution claims 188
Collision claims and limitation actions 188
Service of the writ 189

Submission to the jurisdiction 189
A. Through procedural steps 189
B. Through submission before the court 190

Remedies available 190
A. On the merits 190
B. Provisional remedies—the "Mareva" injunction 190

County court jurisdiction 191

CHAPTER 10. ENFORCEMENT OF MARITIME CLAIMS BY AN ACTION
"IN REM" 193

1. Availability of the action "in rem" 193
Claims specified by The Supreme Court Act 1981 193
(a) Specified claims 193
(b) Maritime liens (s.21(3)) 194
(c) The "sweeping up" clause (s.20(1)(c)) 194
(d) Damage received by a ship (s.20(2)(d)) 194

2. Actions "in rem" and specified categories of claim 195
(i) Action "in rem" in relation to claims within s.20(2)(e)–(r) 195
A. Against the particular ship 195
(a) Legislative history and present scope 196
The reform that did not succeed 196
Reforms that were made—extension to demise chartered ships 197
(b) The critical "in personam" link points 198
"When the cause of action arose" 198
"When the action is brought" 198
"The beneficial owner" 199
The corporate owner—piercing the veil? 199
The effect of long-term financing arrangements 200
"The charterer by demise" 201
B. Against a "sister" ship 201

(a) May an action "in rem" be brought against a sister ship other than that in the
    same ownership as the ship in respect of which the claim arose?   202
    The Administration of Justice Act 1956   202
    The Supreme Court Act 1981   202
(b) If an action "in rem" may be brought in relation to a ship owned by a
    "charterer" does this include time or voyage charterer?   202
(ii) Action "in rem" in relation to claims and questions within s.20(2)(a), (b), (c), (s)   203
(iii) "Maritime lien or other charge" (s.21(3))   203
    The concept of maritime lien   204
    "Or other charge"   204
(iv) The "sweeping up" clause   204

3. Jurisdictional prerequisites other than the Supreme Court Act 1981   205
Link between the issue and England required for an action "in rem" to be brought 205
    The basic rule   205
    The basic rule is qualified   205
    The effect of Conventions   206
    The effect of the Brussels and Lugano Conventions   206

4. Procedure of an action "in rem"   207
Commencement   207
    Service of the writ   208
    Acknowledgment of issue of writ   208
    Acknowledgment of service of writ   208
Amendment of the writ   209
Persons other than defendants   209
Duration of action "in rem"   209

5. The inter-relationship of action "in personam" and action "in rem"   210
Effect of the nature of the action "in rem" on procedure and remedies   210

6. County court jurisdiction   211

CHAPTER 11. DELAY IN SUIT   213

1. Effect of delay   213
Extinguishment of right or remedy?   213
Avoidance of effect of delay   214

2. Aspects of delay   214
1. Effect of foreign time bar   215
  (a) In English proceedings   215
    Prior to Foreign Limitation Periods Act 1984   215
    The Foreign Limitation Periods Act 1984   215
    The Contracts (Applicable Law) Act 1990   215
  (b) Staying English proceedings   216
    (i) Jurisdiction agreement   216
    (ii) Forum non conveniens   216
2. Notice of the claim   217
3. Commencement of suit—issue of writ   217
  Statutory time limits   217
    The general pattern   217
    Limitation periods for particular types of claim   218

The limitation framework   219
  (i) Statutes specifying particular limitation periods for particular types of claim   219
    Carriage claims—Carriage of Goods by Sea Act 1971—The Hague-Visby Rules,
      Art. III(6)   219
    "Collision" claims   221
    Salvage claims—The Merchant Shipping (Salvage and Pollution) Act 1994 Sch. 1
      (as from 1 January 1996 the Merchant Shipping Act 1995 Sch. 11)   222
  (ii) The general pattern—the Limitation Act 1980   222
    Three-year period   223
    Six-year period   223
    Twelve-year period   223
New claims in pending actions   224
Principles outside the Limitation Act   225
  (i) Application by analogy   225
  (ii) Delay—laches   226
4. Delay in service of writ   226
5. Delay in complying with procedural requirements   227
6. Want of prosecution of a claim   227
7. Delay in assertion of the remedy   229
  Judgment on order on the merits   229
  Provisional remedies   229

CHAPTER 12. RESTRICTIONS ON JURISDICTION   231

The Brussels and Lugano Conventions—"multiple proceedings"   231
  "To avoid the risk of irreconcilable judgments"   232
  Scope of "multiple proceedings" provisions   232
    Articles 21, 22 and "exclusive jurisdiction"   232
    As between non-exclusive jurisdictions   233
    Provisional measures   233
    The power or duty to decline jurisdiction   234
      Consideration of the jurisdiction of the foreign court   234
      "Seised" of an action   234
      Multi defendants   235
      The same cause of action and between the same parties (Article 21)   236
        An action in personam and an action in rem   237
        Between the same parties   237
      Related actions (Article 22)   238
        Liability and limitation proceedings   239
      Multiple "exclusive" jurisdiction (Article 23)   239

Restrictions on English proceedings other than under the Brussels or Lugano
Conventions   239
1. Foreign forum agreements   240
  Construction of the clause   240
    Litigation or arbitration   241
  Scope of the clause   241
    Whether the clause is "exclusive"   242
  Limitations on agreements as a jurisdiction base   243
    The Hague and Hague-Visby Rules   243
  The effect in English law   245
    (a) Stay of proceedings   245

The relevance of the foreign law   247
The time bar   248
  (b) Arrest   248
2. Arbitration agreements   249
Arrest and arbitration clauses   249
3. The appropriate forum—"forum conveniens"   250
Concurrent proceedings   253
Limitation of liability   253
Restraint of any foreign proceedings following refusal of stay of English proceedings   254
Jurisdiction agreements   254
4. Issue estoppel and cause of action estoppel   255
5. Sovereign immunity   256
  A. Foreign governments   256
    The general framework   256
      The law prior to 22 November 1978   256
      State Immunity Act 1978   257
        Maritime claims   259
  B. Government of the United Kingdom   260
    "Crown" liability "in personam"   260
    "Crown" liability "in rem"   261
    The "Crown" and "Crown property"   262
      (i) The Crown   262
        (a) The Crown Proceedings Act 1947 and Supreme Court Act 1981   262
        (b) The pre-statute framework   262
      (ii) Crown property   262
        (a) Ships   262
        (b) Cargo and other property—"belonging to the Crown"   263
6. Restrictions on specific types of claims   263
  (i) Nuclear activities   263
  (ii) Trespass to foreign land   264
  (iii) The Rhine Navigation Convention 1868   264
  (iv) Foreign ships   265
    Wages actions   265
    Actions on contracts of service of master or crew   266
    Title to or possession of a foreign ship   266
  (v) Trade disputes—immunity from suit in tort   266
  (vi) Insurance contracts—lack of enforceability   267
7. Abuse of process   267

Restrictions on foreign proceedings   268
Interim relief proceedings   270
Protection of Trading Interests Act 1980   271

CHAPTER 13. ARBITRATION   273

English law and international agreements   273
The UNCITRAL Model Law—transnational arbitration   273
The New York Convention on the Recognition and Enforcement of Foreign Arbitral
  Awards 1958   274

Arbitration and litigation   275
Jurisdiction to decide the validity of an arbitration agreement   276

The law to be applied 277
The law governing substantive matters 277
The law governing procedure (the curial law) 278
Enforceability of arbitration agreements in English law 278
The arbitration agreements, the substantive contract and separability 278
Stay of court proceedings 279
The non-domestic agreement 280
The domestic agreement 281

The English statutory framework—the Arbitration Acts 1950 and 1979 281
The general framework 281
Powers of English courts in respect of arbitration proceedings 282
Inherent supervisory jurisdiction? 282
Interim relief 282
Jurisdictional prerequisite of connection with England? 283
Arrest 284
Review of and appeal to courts from arbitration decisions 284
Exclusion agreements 286

Delay in arbitration proceedings 287
In commencement of proceedings 287
Power in court to extend periods fixed by arbitration agreement 288
Extension of time and summary judgment 289
Delay in prosecution of proceedings 290

The arbitration award and its enforcement 291
English arbitration awards 291
Foreign arbitration awards 291

PART III. INTERIM RELIEF

CHAPTER 14. NATURE AND BASIS OF INTERIM RELIEF 295

Types of relief and procedure 295
In favour of the plaintiff 295
In favour of the defendant 295
1. In favour of the plaintiff 295
(i) The obtaining of evidence 296
(ii) Controlling of actions of parties prior to hearing 297
(iii) Measures against dissipation of defendant's assets 298
Preservation of property 298
"Mareva" injunction 298
Arrest of ship, cargo or freight 299
(iv) Substantive remedy prior to hearing on merits 299
Procedure for obtaining of interim relief by plaintiff 300
Arrest 300
Other modes of interim relief 300
2. In favour of the defendant 301
(i) Security for costs 301
Ease of enforcement of costs order in foreign jurisdiction where plaintiff resident abroad 301

(ii) Requirement of undertaking or counter security   302
Interim relief in arbitration proceedings   302

Effect of the Brussels and Lugano Conventions   303
In favour of the plaintiff   303
  Provisional measures   303
    Effect of other Conventions (Articles 24 and 57)   304
    Multiple proceedings (Articles 24 and Articles 21–23)   304
  Implementation in English law   305
    (i) Interim relief other than arrest or obtaining of evidence   306
    (ii) Arrest in English law   306
      Is it a provisional measure?   306
      Arrest in English law and the Brussels Convention   307
      Arrest and arbitration and the Brussels Convention   308
In favour of the defendant   308
  (i) Security for costs   308
  (ii) Requirement of undertaking or counter security   309

Measures after judgment   309
The Brussels and Lugano Conventions   310

CHAPTER 15. ARREST AND ALTERNATIVE SECURITY   311

Introduction   311
The three functions of arrest   311
  The civil law approach   311
  The approach in English law   311
Alternative security   312

The international scene   312
Convention Relating to the Arrest of Sea-Going Ships 1952   313
  Introduction of Arrest Convention directly into English law through the Brussels and
      Lugano Conventions?   314
    Arrest as a jurisdiction base   314
    Arrest as a provisional measure   315
    Ships which may be arrested   315
The Collision (Civil Jurisdiction) Convention 1952   316
The Hamburg Rules 1978   316
Convention on the Contract for the International Carriage of Goods By Road 1956
    (the CMR)   318
Conventions relating to limitation of liability 1924, 1957 and 1976   319
Summary   319

The arrest framework in English law   320
Arrest and the action "in rem"   320
Arrest as "security"   320
  Bankruptcy or company liquidation   321
    Bankruptcy   321
    Liquidation of companies   321
Property liable to arrest   321
Warrant of arrest and writ "in rem"   322
Stage in proceedings when arrest available   324
Restrictions on availability of arrest   325

(a) Restrictions specifically imposed   325
   Caveat against arrest   325
   Government ships and other property   326
      Foreign governments   326
      Crown ships and other property   326
      Foreign ships or other property   326
   Abuse of process   327
(b) Consequences of lack of jurisdiction on merits   327
   Assertion of jurisdiction "in rem"   327
      The issue of the writ   327
      Ground of challenge to issue of a writ   328
      Staying or dismissal of proceedings   328
   Problem areas—arbitration and foreign jurisdiction   328
      The Civil Jurisdiction and Judgments Act 1982, s.26   329
         The scope of s.26   330
         A plaintiff's right to stay   331
         Cross undertaking for damages   331
(c) Foreign arrest   331
   Arrest in England following a foreign arrest   332
Arrest procedure   332
   The warrant of arrest   332
   Admiralty Marshal's fees and expenses   333
      Undertaking to pay   333
      Where there is more than one arrest   334
   Arrester's expenses   334
   Rights and liabilities in respect of property under or affected by arrest   335
      Third parties   336
         Rights existing at or before arrest   336
         Intervention in proceedings   336
         Expenses of discharge of cargo   337
"Wrongful" arrest   337
   Termination of arrest—release   338
      Limitation of liability and release from arrest   339
         The 1957 Convention and its implementation   339

Judicial sale   340

Security alternative to arrest   340
Caveat against release from arrest or of proceeds of sale   341
   Liability in damages of caveat holder   341
Security in substitution for arrest   341
   Bail, payment into court, guarantee   341
      Bail   342
         Bail and jurisdiction   343
         Release of property arrested   344
         Rearrest   344
         Foreign bail in respect of English proceedings   344
         English bail in respect of foreign proceedings   345
      Payment into court   345
      Guarantee or undertaking   345

Arrest and detention under legislative powers   346

Arrest and execution of judgment   346

CHAPTER 16. THE "MAREVA" INJUNCTION 347

Nature and purpose 347

Roots and development 348
English and foreign elements 349
  The place of the proceedings 349
    (a) Proceedings initiated in an English court 349
      Jurisdiction "in personam" 349
        Need for accrued cause of action 350
        Interim orders in arbitration proceedings 350
        Service out of the jurisdiction and "Mareva" injunction 350
      Jurisdiction "in rem" 351
    (b) Foreign proceedings 351
English and foreign based defendants 352
English and foreign assets 352
  Type of assets 352
  Place of assets 353

Requirement of an undertaking by plaintiff in damages and expenses 355
Damages 355
Expenses 357
Other proceedings 357

Case to be made by the plaintiff 357
Risk of dissipation of assets and likely default 359
  Permitted use of assets 359

Ancillary orders in aid of the injunction 360

Effect of the injunction 361
In relation to the defendant 361
In relation to third parties 362
  The "knowledge" required for breach 362
  Limitation on restrictions of action of third party by injunction 363
  Effect of injunction on third party as grounds for refusal to grant 363

The form of the order—the "maximum sum" approach 363
The standard forms 1994 364

Comparison of arrest and "Mareva" injunction as provisional remedies—a summary 364

PART IV. SECURITY ON THE MERITS—THE LIEN CONCEPT

CHAPTER 17. NATURE AND DEVELOPMENT OF LIENS 369

1. The nature of a "lien"—or what's in a word? 369
Lien and mortgage 369
Lien and charge 370
  The floating charge 370

2. Development of liens in English law   371
A. Common law, equity and statute   371
  The possessory lien   371
  The equitable lien   371
  The statutory lien   372
B. Admiralty   372
  Applicability of liens of common law, equity and statute   372
  Admiralty liens—the maritime lien and statutory lien   372

3. Which lien and when?   372
One lien or more?   373
Priorities   374

4. Foreign liens   374

5. Liens and the registration of interests   374

6. Insolvency and liens   375
1. Companies   375
  Winding up or liquidation   375
  Administration orders   375
2. Individuals—bankruptcy   376

7. Maritime liens, statutory liens in Admiralty and the action "in rem"   376
  The action in rem and action in personam   377
1. The categories of claim enforceable by action "in rem"   378
2. The Supreme Court Act 1981 and the action "in rem"   378
  (i) Claims based on maritime lien (s.21(3))   378
  (ii) Claims based on s.20(2)(a)–(c), (s)   378
  (iii) Claims within the sweeping up clause (s.20(1)(c))   378
  (iv) Claims based on s.20(2)(e)–(r)   379
3. Remaining uncertainties of the action "in rem"   379
4. Lien and the action "in rem"   379
  (i) Historical development of the action in rem   379
    Procedure   379
    Personification   380
    A third view—hypothec and deodand   381
  (ii) Current factors of substance and procedure   381
    Substance   381
    Procedure   382
  (iii) The views, the flaws in them and liens   382

CHAPTER 18. MARITIME LIENS   387

1. Claims to which a maritime lien may attach   387

2. Consequences of attracting a maritime lien   387

3. The nature of the maritime lien   389
I. The maritime lien and the action "in rem"   389
II. The "maritime lien" as a legal category of claims   389
  At the time of "The Bold Buccleugh"—in 1851   390

III. The modern maritime lien and statutory lien in Admiralty compared   391
IV. The maritime lien—procedure or substance?   391
  "The Bold Buccleugh"   392
  Modern views of "The Bold Buccleugh"   393

4. Assets subject to a maritime lien   394
I. A ship   395
  Things that go upon the water   395
  A ship, its parts and things on board   395
  The ship's apparel and salvage claims   397
II. Other property   397
  (a) Freight   398
  (b) Cargo   398
    Bottomry and respondentia   399
    Salvage   399

5. Enforceability of maritime liens   399
Procedure or personification   399
Different aspect of enforceability   400
  (i) Enforceability of the claim "in personam"   400
  (ii) Enforceability against other creditors   400
  (iii) Enforceability against purchasers   400
  (iv) Enforceability against asset when the present owner is not liable "in personam"   401
    (a) The differing contexts in which the lack of personal liability of the shipowner
        arises   401
      (i) Government ships   401
      (ii) Transfer of control by agreement   401
      (iii) Involuntary transfer   402
    (b) A general principle of shipowner's liability?   402
    The concept of the owner's authority   403
    Liability of the shipowner rather than the ship as a general principle 403
    (c) The different claims and the development of the need for the shipowner's
        liability   404
    Damage   404
    Master's disbursements   405
    Salvage   405
    Wages   406
    Bottomry   407

6. Transferability of maritime liens   407
I. Voluntary transfer   408
  (i) Assignment   408
    Bottomry bonds   408
    Maritime liens apart from bottomry bonds   408
    (a) General principles of assignability   408
    (b) Maritime lien principles of assignability   409
      Restrictions on assignment of wages   410
  (ii) Subrogation   410
  (iii) Voluntary payment of claims   411
II. Involuntary transfer   411
  (i) Bankruptcy and death   411
  (ii) Statutory right to contribution   411

7. Extinction of maritime liens 412

I. Immunity from suit 412

  Foreign states 412

  The United Kingdom Government 412

II. Delay of suit 412

III. Effect of stay of proceedings 413

  Effect on maritime lien attached to property the target for the action 413

  Arbitration, foreign jurisdiction clause or *forum non conveniens* stay 413

    Effect on maritime lien attached to property retained 413

    Equivalent security 414

IV. Lodging of bail or provision of other security 414

  (a) Bail 414

    Limitation of liability—limitation action 414

  (b) Payment into court 415

  (c) Security by way of guarantee or undertaking 415

V. Bankruptcy and liquidation 416

  Bankruptcy 416

  Winding up or liquidation 416

VI. Agreement, waiver and estoppel 416

VII. Destruction of the property 417

VIII. Judgment on liability 417

IX. Judicial sale 417

8. The international framework relating to maritime liens 418

I. The Convention of 1926 419

  Mortgages 419

  Maritime liens 419

  Other liens 420

II. The Convention of 1967 420

  Principal changes from the Convention of 1926 420

  The pattern of the Convention 421

    Mortgage and hypotheques 421

    Maritime liens 421

    Other liens 422

III. The Convention of 1993 422

  The pattern of the Convention 423

    Registration of vessels 423

    Registered mortgages hypotheques and "registrable charges" 423

    "Maritime liens and right of retention" 423

    The liens follow the vessel 424

    Other liens 425

CHAPTER 19. STATUTORY LIENS IN ADMIRALTY 427

The action "in rem" and statutory liens in Admiralty 427

1. Nature of the "statutory lien" 427

I. Origins and early development 427

  Admiralty Court Acts 1840 and 1861 and maritime liens 428

  Statutory extensions of the action "in rem" between 1861 and 1925 428

II. The Supreme Court Act 1981—the present framework for the action "in rem" 428

III. "The statutory lien in Admiralty"—is it to be equated with the action "in rem"?   429
  (a) The action "in rem"—substance and procedure   429
  (b) The nature of the claims attracting the action "in rem"   430
      (i) Claims in s.20(2)(e)–(r)—the proprietary role of the action "in rem"   431
      (ii) Claims in s.20(2)(a)(b)(c) and (s)—the procedural role of the action "in rem"   431
      (iii) Claims within s.20(1)(c)—past jurisdiction   432
IV. Summary   433
  (i) The need for precise analysis   433
  (ii) The need for legislative clarification   433
    (a) Priority   433
    (b) Enforceability against third parties   434

2. Creation of the lien   434

3. Assets subject to the lien   435
I. Claims under s.21(4)   435
II. Claims under s.21(2) or s.20(1)(c)   435

4. Transferability   436

5. Termination   436

6. The legal consequences of attracting the action "in rem"—a summary   436

CHAPTER 20. POSSESSORY LIENS   439

Nature of a possessory lien   439

Assets subject to the lien   439

A. Common law possessory liens (applying to but not created primarily in maritime
    law)   440
1. Generally applicable principles   440
  (i) Commencement of the lien   440
    A contractual right to a possessory lien   440
  (ii) Enforceability of the lien   441
    (a) Against creditors or liquidator   441
    (b) Against third parties other than creditors   441
      Successors in title   441
      Present owners   441
      Enforcement of the lien   442
    (c) The effect of insolvency   442
      Company insolvency   442
      Individual insolvency   443
  (iii) Termination of the lien   443
    (a) Loss of possession   443
    (b) Taking of action inconsistent with a possessory lien   443
    (c) Tender of amount due   444
2. General liens   444
  (a) By usage   444
    Claims to which a general lien may attach   444
    Enforceability of the lien   444
  (b) By contract   445
  (c) By statute   445
3. Particular liens   445

(a) By usage   445
    Claims to which a particular lien attaches   445
       (i) Obligation to accept goods   446
       (ii) Work done on a chattel   446
       The shiprepairer/shipbuilder   446
       (iii) Agent's lien   446
       (iv) Co-owner's lien   447
    Enforceability of the lien   447
(b) By contract   447
(c) By statute   447

B. Maritime possessory liens   448
Maritime and other possessory liens   448
Claims to which maritime possessory liens attach by usage   448
Enforceability, enforcement and termination   448
    Enforcement of the lien   449
The individual liens   449
    (i) The shipowner's lien on cargo for freight   449
    Continued existence after delivery of possession to warehouse   449
    Termination   450
    Sale of landed goods   450
    (ii) Shipowner's lien for average contributions   451
       (a) General average   451
       (b) Particular average   451
    (iii) The salvor's lien   451
    Agent's lien   451
    (iv) Warehouseman's lien for wharf or warehouse charges   451
    (v) The broker's lien   452
    Enforceability   452
    (vi) Harbour and other public authorities   453
    Statutory rights of detention   453
    Need to detain   453
    The power of sale   453
    The effect of company insolvency   454

CHAPTER 21. EQUITABLE LIENS   455

1. The substance of the lien   455
Equitable lien and equitable charge   455
    The floating charge   456
Reservation of title clause   456

2. The equitable lien in Admiralty   456

3. Creation of the lien   457
I. By contract   457
    Bills of Sale Acts 1878 and 1882   457
    Companies Act 1985   457
    Shipowner's lien on subfreight   458
II. Arising from the relationship of the parties   458
    Vendor's lien for unpaid purchase money   458

III. Arising from a course of conduct   458

4. Enforceability of the lien   459
I. Against third parties   459
II. Tracing into other assets   459

5. Transferability   460

6. Termination   460

CHAPTER 22. CREATING A LIEN BY CONTRACT   461

1. The lien clause—general considerations   461
Common clauses   461
Multi-lien clauses   462
   The New York Produce Exchange Charterparty   462
   The Baltime Charterparty   463
   The Gencon Charterparty   464
The lien clause in context   464

2. The liens created   464
I. Owner's lien on cargo   464
  (a) Nature of lien   464
  (b) The cargo   465
II. Owner's lien on subfreights or sub-hire   466
  (a) Nature of the lien   466
   The content of the right   467
  (b) Does "freight" include charterparty hire?   467
  (c) Are "sub-subfreights" and "sub-subcharter hire" included? 467
III. Charterer's lien on ship   468
  Nature of the lien   468
IV. Lien not to be suffered or permitted to continue   468

3. Charterer's liability dependent on exercise of owner's lien—the "cesser clause"   468

4. The need for registration   469

5. The governing law   469

CHAPTER 23. PRIORITIES   471

I. The general problems of priority   471

II. Principles of priority in English law   472
1. The basic principles of "in personam" priority   472
  Legal and equitable interests   472
  Other modifications   472
  Maritime claims "in personam"   473
2. The Admiralty rules of priority "in rem"   473
  "In rem" priority categories   474
  "In personam" priority principles in the "in rem" framework 474
3. Priority between "in rem" and "in personam" claims   474

III. The priority structure of English law 475
1. Title (or ownership) 475
  "In personam" priority—the basic rules 475
   (i) Equitable interests 475
    (a) Creation of beneficial title through a trust 475
    Reservation of title 475
    (b) Contract of sale—transfer of equitable title 476
   (ii) Other modifications of "first in time" 476
    (a) Registration provisions 476
     (i) The Bills of Sale Act 1878 476
     (ii) Merchant Shipping Act 1995 477
      The registration provisions 478
       Private law consequences from public law benefits 479
       Priorities 479
       Registrability, registration, legal and equitable interests 480
       Statutory powers of owners of small ships and fishing vessels 481
       The need for clarification 481
    (b) Statutory provisions relating to priority of title. Sale of Goods Act 1979 and Factors Act 1889 481
  "In rem" priority 481
2. Use for a specified period of time 482
  (i) Charterparty 482
   "In personam" priority 482
   "In rem" priority 482
   The effect of registration 482
  (ii) Lease or bailment of goods 483
   "In personam" priority 483
   "In rem" priority 483
   The effect of registration 483
3. Security interests 483
  A. General principles 484
   "In personam" priority 484
   Registration provisions 484
    The Bills of Sale Acts 1878 and 1882 484
    The Companies Act 1985 485
    The Companies Act 1989 486
     English and overseas companies 486
     Notice of crystallization of floating charge 488
   "In rem" priority 488
  B. Priority and each security interest 488
   1. Mortgage 488
    (i) Mortgage of ships 488
     (a) Registrability of mortgage 488
     A registered ship 489
     An unregistered ship 489
     (b) Effect on "in personam" priority 490
     In registered ships 490
     In unregistered ships 491
     (c) Foreign mortgages 491
     (d) "In rem" priority 492
    (ii) Mortgage of cargo 492

"In personam" priority	492
"In rem" priority	492
(iii) Mortgage of freight or charterparty hire or insurance moneys	493
"In personam" priority	493
Creation	493
Enforceability	493
Admiralty jurisdiction	493
"In rem" priority	493
(iv) Bottomry and/or respondentia	494
2. Charges	494
Equitable charge—nature	494
Charging orders	494
"Mareva" injunction	494
"In personam" priority—the structure	494
Floating charge	494
"In rem" priority	495
3. Pledge	495
"In personam" priority	495
Priority as against other interests	495
Priority issues between pledgees	496
"In rem" priority	496
4. Liens	496
1. "In personam" priority	496
(A) "Statutory" liens	496
Solicitor's statutory lien	496
(B) The possessory lien	496
(a) As against interests other than a possessory lien	496
Rights of unpaid seller of goods	497
Statutory rights of detention and sale	497
(b) As between possessory liens	497
(C) The equitable lien	498
(D) The "Mareva" injunction	498
2. "In rem" priority	498
(a) Priority between the categories of liens	498
(i) Maritime liens	498
(ii) Possessory liens	499
(iii) Statutory liens in Admiralty	499
Mortgage and charges	499
(i) Registered mortgage	499
(ii) Unregistered mortgage	500
(iii) Equitable charge and equitable lien	500
Statutory liens other than mortgage or charge claims	500
(b) Priority within each category of lien	501
A. Maritime liens	501
General principles	501
The particular liens	502
(i) The damage lien	502
(ii) The salvage lien	502
(iii) Wages lien	502
(iv) Disbursements lien	503
(v) Bottomry	503

B. Statutory liens 504
    1. Mortgage or charge 504
       (i) Mortgage of ships 504
       (ii) Mortgage of cargo 505
       (iii) Mortgage of freight or charterparty hire 505
          The right of an assignee of freight 505
       (iv) Equitable charge and equitable lien 505
    2. Ownership claims 505
       Beneficial ownership 506
    3. Statutory liens in Admiralty other than those based on ownership, mortgage
       or charge 506
       (i) As between different liens 506
       (ii) As between liens of the same class 506

**IV. Priority relationship between actions "in rem" and "in personam" proprietary
    interests** 506
1. Ownership 507
2. Mortgage, charge and lien 508
3. Interests created by statute 508
   Statutory rights of port authorities to detention and sale of ships 508
   Solicitor's lien under the Solicitors Act 1974 509
   Limitation funds 509
4. The execution creditor 509
   A charging order 510
5. Effect of judicial sale in action "in rem" 511
6. Summary 511

V. Attempts at international frameworks—mortgages and liens 511

PART V. REMEDIES

CHAPTER 24. LIMITATION OF LIABILITY 515

The general principle 515
The link between liability and limitation proceedings 516

International limitation frameworks 517
Global limitation 517
Limitation for particular claims in addition to "global" limitation 518
   Carriage Conventions 518
   Mortgages and liens Conventions 519
   Other relevant Conventions 519

Limitation of liability in English law 520
The general pattern 520
   Claims subject to limitation 520
   Claiming limitation 520
1. Global limitation 521
   The 1976 Convention 522
      Applicability of the Convention 523
      Courts in which limitation may be claimed 523

Persons entitled to limit liability   524
Claims within the Convention   524
"Breaking the limits" (Article 4)   525
The limitation amounts   526
The Limitation Fund   526
  Consequences of establishing a fund   527
  Effect on liability jurisdiction—release of security   527
Application of the 1976 Convention in United Kingdom laws   527
"Limitation actions"   528
  Prior to 1 December 1986   528
  From 1 December 1986   528
  The procedure   530
  The Limitation Fund   530
Discretion in establishing or exercising jurisdiction   531
  1. Service of writ out of the jurisdiction   531
    Prior to the 1979 Act   531
      The discretion of the court in granting leave   532
    Effect of the 1979 Act   533
  2. Stay of proceedings   533
    (a) The 1976 Convention, jurisdiction agreements and forum interest   533
    (b) Forum non conveniens   534
      Effect of the 1976 Limitation Convention   535
  3. Effect of the Brussels and Lugano Conventions on jurisdiction (as amended)   536
    (a) The service of the writ out of England   536
    (b) Staying proceedings   537
The law applicable to limitation issues   537
Recognition of foreign limitation decrees   539
  The Brussels and Lugano Conventions   539
2. Oil pollution claims   540
  (a) Claiming limitation   540
    The limitation action   540
      Stay of proceedings   541
        The "Limitation Fund" and the consequences of constituting such a fund   541
        Limitation Funds outside the United Kingdom   542
      The applicable law   542
      Recognition of foreign judgment   542
    Global limitation and oil pollution limitation compared   542
  (b) Limited liability of the International Fund for Compensation for Oil Pollution 542
    Jurisdiction, applicable law and recognition of judgments   543
  (c) Effect of the Brussels and Lugano Conventions   543
3. The Pilotage Act 1987   543
  Claiming limitation   544
  Jurisdiction, applicable law and recognition of judgments   544
4. Dock and canal owners, harbour and conservancy authorities   545

CHAPTER 25. REMEDIES IN ACTIONS ON THE MERITS   547

Finality of litigation—the effect of a judgment or arbitration award   547

Remedies generally and in Admiralty   548
  Remedies and grounds   548

1. The remedy awarded   548
   The general pattern   548
     Jurisdiction over remedies   548
     Remedies in actions "in personam"   549
     Remedies in actions "in rem"   549
   Types of remedies   550
     Actions "in personam"   550
       (i) Payment of money   550
      Grounds of the remedy   550
      Judgments in foreign currency   550
      Interest on debts and damages   551
       (ii) Orders other than for the payment of money   552
      Proprietary relief   552
       Tracing   552
      Enforcement of contracts and other acts   552
      Termination of contracts—rescission and recognition of repudiation   552
      Enforcement of arbitral agreements and awards   553
       (iii) Prohibition or restraint of acts—injunctions   553
       (iv) Compensatory orders   553
       (v) Declaratory orders   553
     Actions "in rem"   554
     Judicial sale   554
       (A) General powers   554
       (B) Property under arrest   554
     Remedies "in personam"   555
       (A) Damages   556
       (B) Equitable remedies   556
2. Enforcement of judgments of English courts   556
   Judgment for money payment   557
   Judgment other than for money payment   558

PART VI. FOREIGN LAW

CHAPTER 26. APPLICATION OF FOREIGN LAW   561

I. The English approach   561
1. The three stage process   561
   The operation of English "public policy" on foreign legislation   562
2. Limitations on the selection process   563
   (a) The scope of the dispositive rule   563
     Substantive limitation   563
     Statutory provisions—is a connecting link required?   563
   (b) The mandatory dispositive rule   564
   (c) Foreign law deemed to be English law   565
3. Choice of law and jurisdiction   565
   (a) Discretionary jurisdiction—relevance of governing law   565
   (b) Statutory claims   566
4. Maritime claims and the English choice of law process   566
   The problem of the high seas   566

Classification of maritime claims   567
Statutory claims—Admiralty jurisdiction and choice of law   567

II. Alternative approaches to selection by classification qualified by public policy   568

III. The categories and their selection rules   569
1. Substance or procedure   569
   (a) Time bars   570
   (b) Priorities   570
      The role of the law of the forum   571
      Maritime claims   571
   (c) Remedies   572
   (d) Limitation of liability   572
   (e) Evidence   573
2. Choice of law for substantive issues   573
   (a) Contract   574
      The law apart from the 1990 Act   575
         The proper law of the contract   575
         The ambit of the proper law   575
            Matters of formation—agreement, formality, capacity   576
               The "putative proper law"   576
            Illegality   577
            The primacy of the parties' choice and its limitations on the parties' choice   577
               (i) The forum mandatory rule   577
               (ii) Public policy   578
         Where there is no selection—"closest and most real connection"   578
         Jurisdiction or arbitration agreement   578
            Selection of law and jurisdiction   578
            Validity of the clause   579
            Content of arbitration and jurisdiction clauses   580
               (a) Arbitration clause   580
               (b) Jurisdiction clause   581
      The Contracts (Applicable Law) Act 1990   581
      Matters excluded from the Convention   582
      Matters within the Convention   583
      The Convention rules   583
         Aspects of contracts subject to applicable law   583
         Laws to be applied in addition to or substitution for the law generally applicable   584
            Third party rights   584
            Subrogation   584
         "Mandatory rules"   584
         "Ordre public" (Article 16)   585
            The choice of the parties (Article 3)   585
            The law generally applicable where there is no choice (Article 4)   586
               Exceptions to the general presumption   586
               Performance characteristic of the contract   587
                  The rebuttable presumptions   587
   (b) Tort   588
      (i) Torts committed in England   588
      (ii) Torts committed on the high seas   588
         (a) Acts occurring on board one ship   588

(b) More than one ship involved 589
(iii) Torts committed on foreign land or waters—prior to 1969 589
Boys v. Chaplin and its consequences 590
Statutory reform 591
The forum mandatory rule 592
The context of the applicable English law 592
Torts on the high seas involving more than one ship 592
Torts in foreign territory or on board a foreign ship 593
English statutory implementation of maritime international provisions 593
(c) Restitution or unjust enrichment 594
The nature of claims within the "category" 594
The governing law 595
Maritime claims—general average and salvage 596
General average 596
(i) Contractual 596
Contract of carriage and adjustment of average 596
Average bond 597
(ii) Unjust enrichment 598
Salvage 598
(i) Contract 598
(ii) Unjust enrichment 598
(d) Proprietary issues 598
General approach 598
Proprietary maritime claims 599
(i) Assertion of a proprietary interest 600
(a) Ship claims 600
Mortgage and sale contracts 600
Liens 601
The decision of "The Halcyon Isle" 601
The effect of the decision 602
Rationale of the decision 602
(i) Jurisdiction 602
(ii) Procedure or remedy 603
The issue in the case 603
The desirable approach 603
Chartering of ships 603
(b) Cargo claims and (c) Money claims 604
(ii) Transfer of a proprietary interest 604
Assertion, transfer and priority 605

Summary 605

CHAPTER 27. ENFORCEMENT OF FOREIGN JUDGMENTS AND ARBITRAL AWARDS OUTSIDE THE BRUSSELS AND LUGANO CONVENTIONS 607

1. Foreign judgments 607
Application of merger and issue estoppel 607
Competing foreign judgments 609
Recognition and enforcement 609
Judgments of other United Kingdom courts 610
(a) Recognition 610
(b) Enforcement 610
General effect of registration 611

Costs, expenses and interest 611
Money provisions of judgments (Schedule 6) 611
Staying of enforcement proceedings (Schedule 6, para. 9) 611
Setting aside of registration (Schedule 6, para. 10) 612
Non-money provisions (Schedule 7) 612
The registration process 612
Judgments of courts other than of the United Kingdom 613
(i) Recognition and enforcement without registration 613
Judgments "in personam" and "in rem" 613
Judgments in actions "in rem" 613
When is a judgment "in rem"? 613
Prerequisites for and defences to recognition and enforcement 614
Foreign court jurisdiction 615
Judgments "in personam" 615
Presence 615
Submission 616
Judgments in proceedings brought contrary to agreement 616
Recognition and enforcement 617
Recognition 617
Enforcement 617
Judgments "in rem" 617
Recognition and enforcement of judgments "in rem" 617
Recognition 617
Enforcement 618
(ii) Recognition and enforcement through registration 618
Courts of specified Commonwealth countries 618
Courts of specified countries 618
Foreign Judgments (Reciprocal Enforcement) Act 1933 618
Statutes adapting the Foreign Judgments (Reciprocal Enforcement) Act 1933 619
Restrictions on enforcement of foreign judgments 619
Protection of trade 619
Judgments against states 620
(a) Against "the United Kingdom" in overseas countries 620
(b) Against states other than the United Kingdom 621

II. Arbitral awards 621
As between parts of the United Kingdom 621
Awards made outside the United Kingdom 621
(a) Without registration 621
(b) Through registration 622

CHAPTER 28. JUDGMENTS AND SETTLEMENTS WITHIN THE
BRUSSELS OR LUGANO CONVENTION 625

I. The general pattern 625
Judgments 625
The link between recognition and enforcement 626
"Authentic instruments" and court settlements 626

II. Judgments within the Convention 627
"Civil or commercial matters" 627

Connection with a member State   627
Types of judgments   627
  Judgments in action "in rem"   627
  "Ex parte" orders   628
  Ancillary or procedural orders   628
    Procedure or substance—who controls?   629
  Judgments on judgments   629
  Judgments within other Conventions given precedence   630
    Maritime Conventions within Article 57   631
      The CMR   631
      The Oil Pollution Conventions 1969 and 1971   632
      The Maritime Liens and Mortgage Conventions 1926, 1967 and 1993   632
    Conventions on liability in respect of nuclear incidents   632

III. The jurisdiction of the recognizing or enforcing court   632

IV. Grounds of non-recognition or non-enforcement   633
Relevance of jurisdiction of adjudicating court   633
  Judgments based on the extended "exorbitant" jurisdiction set out in Article 3
    (Article 59)   634
2. Grounds other than jurisdiction of the adjudicating court   635
  Grounds common to Brussels and Lugano Conventions   635
    (i) Public policy (Article 27(1))   635
    (ii) The defendant's opportunity to put his case (Article 27(2))   637
      Connection with like jurisdiction requirement   637
      The requirements of Article 27(2)   638
        "Duly served"   638
        Sufficient time for preparation of defence   639
        The scope for enquiry by the enforcement court   639
        The relevance of the defendant's conduct or acts   640
        The document instituting the proceedings   641
    (iii) Irreconcilability of judgments (Article 27(3), 27(5))   642
      "Irreconcilable"   642
        (A) Judgment of a court of the enforcement State (Article 27(3))   643
        (B) Judgment of a court of a non-contracting State (Article 27(5))   643
    (iv) Preliminary status questions (Article 27(4))   643

V. The recognition and enforcement process   643
Recognition as an incidental issue   643
The enforcement process   644
  The ex parte application (Articles 31 to 33, 46, 47)   645
    Security for costs   645
    Documentary support required   646
  Stay of recognition or enforcement proceedings pending appeal in state of origin 646
    Scope of the provisions   647
    Is the provision for stay "free standing"?   647
      The "ordinary appeal"   648
  The decision on the application for enforcement (or in the United Kingdom,
    registration)   649

VI. Appeals against recognition decision or enforcement declaration   649
1. Protective measures during period for appeal   649
2. Appeal from authorization of enforcement (or leave to register)   649
   Enforcement made conditional on provision of security   650
3. Appeal from refusal of enforcement   651
   The defendant's opportunity to put his case   651
4. Further appeal   652

APPENDICES

APPENDIX 1. STATUTES   653
Administration of Justice Act 1956, ss.45–50 (as amended)   653
Arbitration Act 1975   656
Supreme Court Act 1981 ss.20–24 (as amended)   659
Civil Jurisdiction and Judgments Act 1982   663
Contracts (Applicable Law) Act 1990   714

APPENDIX 2. RULES OF THE SUPREME COURT   729
Order 2, Rule 1   729
Order 6, Rule 8   729
Order 10, Rules 1, 3   730
Order 11, Rules 1, 4, 5   731
Order 12, Rule 8   734
Order 75, Rules 1–17, 21, 22, 37, 37A, 38–40   735

APPENDIX 3. CONVENTIONS
International Convention for the Unification of Certain Rules Relating to the Arrest
     of Sea-Going Ships, Brussels, 10 May 1952   749
International Convention on Certain Rules Concerning Civil Jurisdiction in Matters
     of Collision, Brussels, 10 May 1952   753
International Convention on Maritime Liens and Mortgages 1993   756

APPENDIX 4.
Private International Law (Miscellaneous Provisions) Act 1995, Parts III, IV 763

Index   767

Table of Cases

A *v.* B [1984] 1 All E.R. 265 .... 443, 444
A *v.* B [1989] 2 Lloyd's Rep. 423 350
A *v.* B (X intervening) [1983] 2 Lloyd's Rep. 532 360
A *v.* C [1980] 2 Lloyd's Rep. 200 .... 296, 298, 459
A and B *v.* C (No. 2) [1981] 1 Lloyd's Rep. 559 360
A and B *v.* C and D [1982] 1 Lloyd's Rep. 166 .... 186, 279
AG *v.* Anderson, *The Independent*, 31 March 1988 331
AGF *v.* Chiyoda [1992] 1 Lloyd's Rep. 325 234
AJP Pritt, The [1991] I.L.Pr. 194 (Corte di Appello Genoa) 150
APJ Shalin, The [1991] 2 Lloyd's Rep. 62 .... 333, 338
AS Autoteile Service GmbH *v.* Malhe (220/84) [1986] 3 CMLR 321 (ECJ) 107
A/S Helsingors Sö & Handelscompagnie *v.* Walton (1921) 9 Ll.L.Rep. 105 450
Abidin Daver, The [1983] 3 All E.R. 46 (C.A.); [1984] A.C. 398; [1984] 1 Lloyd's Rep. 339; [1984] 1
    All E.R. 470 (H.L.) 246, 251, 253
Acrux, The [1962] 1 Lloyd's Rep. 405; [1965] P. 391; [1965] 1 Lloyd's Rep. 565 .... 26, 36, 37, 45, 47,
    204, 428, 507, 508, 555, 564, 566, 568, 602
Adah, The (1830) 2 Hag. Adm. 326 44
Adams *v.* Cape Industries plc [1991] 1 All E.R. 929 (C.A.) 176, 200, 614–616
Aden Refinery Co. Ltd *v.* Ugland Management Co. [1986] 2 Lloyd's Rep. 336 285
Adhiguna Meranti, The [1988] 1 Lloyd's Rep. 384; overruled [1994] 3 All E.R. 749 534
Admiralty Commissioners *v.* Valverda (Owners) [1938] A.C. 173 27
Adolf Leonhardt, The [1973] 2 Lloyd's Rep. 318 594
Adolf Warski, The [1976] 1 Lloyd's Rep. 107; [1976] 2 Lloyd's Rep. 241 (C.A.) 216, 246–248, 579
Advanced Portfolio Inc. *v.* Ainsworth, *The Times*, 15 November 1995 269
Aegean Captain, The [1980] 1 Lloyd's Rep. 617 .... 74, 83, 188
Aegnoussiotis, The [1977] 1 Lloyd's Rep. 268 465
Afala, The [1995] 2 Lloyd's Rep. 286 322
Africano, The [1894] P. 141 506
Agence Belgo-Danoise NV *v.* Rederis Hapag Lloyd AG, 25 June 1976, ECD 1–57–B3 133
Agenor, The [1984] LMLN 130 551
Agia Skepi, The [1992] 2 Lloyd's Rep. 467 .... 184, 185
Agios Georgis, The [1978] 2 Lloyd's Rep. 192 465
Agrafax *v.* Scottish Soc. [1995] I.L.Pr. 753 181
Agrebele, The [1979] 2 Lloyd's Rep. 117 352
Agromet Motoimport Ltd *v.* Maulden Engineering Co. (Beds) Ltd [1985] 2 All E.R. 346 288
Aifanourios, The [1980] 2 Lloyd's Rep. 403 .... 60, 62
Akerblom *v.* Price Potter Walker & Co. (1881) 7 Q.B.D. 129 596
Al Battani, The [1993] 2 Lloyd's Rep. 219 .... 245–248, 253
Al Tabith, The [1995] 2 Lloyd's Rep. 336 .... 214, 222
Al Wahab, The [1983] 2 Lloyd's Rep. 365; [1983] 2 All E.R. 884 (H.L.) 575, 576
Alaskan Trader, The [1984] 1 All E.R. 129 553
Albany, The [1983] 2 Lloyd's Rep. 195 222
Albeko Schuhmaschinen *v.* Kamborian Shoe Machine Co. Ltd (1961) 111 L.J. 519 576
Albermarle Supply Co. Ltd *v.* Hind & Co. [1928] 1 K.B. 307 497
Alcom Ltd *v.* Republic of Colombia [1984] 2 All E.R. 6 (H.L.) 258
Aldington Shipping *v.* Bradstock Shipping [1988] 1 Lloyd's Rep. 475 534
Alexander Larsen, The (1841) W. Rob. 288 390

xli

TABLE OF CASES

Alexandros G Tsavlivis, The [1993] LMLN 369 474
Ali Fahd Shoboksha Group v. Moneim, *The Times*, 8 March 1989 359
Aliakmon, The [1978] 2 Lloyd's Rep. 499 (H.L.) 476
Aliakmon, The [1986] 2 Lloyd's Rep. 1; [1986] 2 All E.R. 145 (H.L.) 200, 458
Alina, The (1880) L.R. 5 Ex. D. 227 .... 59, 61
Aline, The (1839) 1 W. Rob. 111 .... 41, 502, 504
Allen v. McAlpine [1968] 2 Q.B. 229 227
Alletta, The [1974] 1 Lloyd's Rep. 40 .... 226, 309, 324, 345
Allied Arab Bank Ltd v. Hajjar [1987] 3 All E.R. 739 361
Allied Arab Bank v. Hajjar, *The Times*, 18 January 1988 347
Allison (Kenneth) Ltd v. Limehouse and Co. [1992] A.C. 105 (H.L.) 174
Allpac Holding BV v. Maier Am Tor [1982] ECC 200 (C.A. Amsterdam) 109
Alltrans Inc. v. Interdom Holdings Ltd [1991] 2 All E.R. 571 (C.A.) 303
Ally, The [1952] 2 Lloyd's Rep. 427 .... 440, 441, 447, 497
Almare Prima, The [1989] 2 Lloyd's Rep. 376 273
Almerck, The [1965] P. 357 222
Amazona and Yayamaria, The [1989] 2 Lloyd's Rep. 130 (C.A.) 220
Amazonia, The [1990] 1 Lloyd's Rep. 236 .... 273, 278, 581
Ambatielos, The and the Cephalonia [1923] P. 68 44
American Cynamid v. Ethicon Ltd [1975] A.C. 396 297
Anangel Friendship, The [1983] Com.L.R. 139 286
Andalina, The (1886) L.R. 12 P.D. 1 398
Andre Theodore, The (1904) 10 Asp. M.L.C. 94 .... 60, 568
Andrea Ursula, The [1973] Q.B. 265; [1971] 1 Lloyd's Rep. 145 .... 197, 265
Andres Bonifaco, The [1994] LMLN 382 (High Ct. Singapore) 200
Andria, The. *See* Vasso, The.
Andrico Unity, The, 1989 (4) S.A. 325 (A) (South Africa) 601
Anema BV v. Broekman Motorships BV [1991] I.L.Pr. 285 (District Ct. Rotterdam) 113
Angel Bell, The [1981] Q.B. 65; [1979] 2 Lloyd's Rep. 491; [1980] 1 Lloyd's Rep. 632 .... 106, 347, 353,
                                                                                          359, 360, 429, 494, 498, 600
Angelic Grace, The [1994] 1 Lloyd's Rep. 168; [1995] 1 Lloyd's Rep. 87 (C.A.) 270, 276, 549
Anichab, The [1921] P. 218 49
Anna H, The [1994] 1 Lloyd's Rep. 287; [1995] 1 Lloyd's Rep. 11 (C.A.) 108, 177, 178, 207, 209, 235,
                                                                                          307, 315, 325, 342, 343
Anna L, The [1994] 2 Lloyd's Rep. 374 224
Annandale, The (1877) 2 P.D. 218 48
Annangel Glory, The [1988] 1 Lloyd's Rep. 45 .... 370, 373, 458, 466, 484, 485, 487, 493
Annett, The [1919] P. 105 266
Antaios, The [1983] 2 Lloyd's Rep. 473 (C.A.); [1985] A.C. 191; [1984] 2 Lloyd's Rep. 235; [1984] 3
  All E.R. 229 (H.L.) 285–287
Antares, The (Nos. 1 and 2) [1987] 1 Lloyd's Rep. 424 (C.A.) 220, 288
Antares Shipping Corpn. v. The Ship Capricorn [1973] F.C. 955 (Fed. Ct. Canada) 556
Anterist v. Credit Lyonnais (22/85) [1987] 1 CMLR 333 (ECJ) 116
Anton Piller KG v. Manufacturing Processes Ltd [1976] Ch. 55 (C.A.) 296
Antonis P. Lemos, The [1984] 1 Lloyd's Rep. 464 (C.A.); [1985] A.C. 711; [1985] 1 Lloyd's Rep. 283
  (H.L.) 21, 58–60, 66, 432, 614
Apex, The [1982] 1 Lloyd's Rep. 476 286
Apple Corpn. v. Apple Computer Inc. [1992] RPC 70 297
Arab African Energy Corpn. Ltd v. Olieprodukten Nederland BV [1983] 2 Lloyd's Rep. 419 286
Arab Monetary Fund v. Hashim [1989] 3 All E.R. 461 296
Arab Monetary Fund v. Hashim (No. 2) [1990] 1 All E.R. 673 .... 296, 361
Arab Monetary Fund v. Hashim (No. 9) [1993] 1 Lloyd's Rep. 543 .... 215, 570
Arantzaru Mendi, The [1939] A.C. 256; 63 Ll.L.Rep. 89 (H.L.) 335
Arctic Explorer, The [1984] AMC 2413 (USA) 538
Arctic Star, The, *The Times*, 5 February 1985 (C.A.) 324, 332, 344, 413
Argenpuma, The [1984] 2 Lloyd's Rep. 563 282
Aries Tanker, Corpn. v. Total Transport Ltd [1977] 1 All E.R. 398 220
Arina, The (1886) 12 P.D. 119 38
Armar, The [1980] 2 Lloyd's Rep. 450; [1981] 1 All E.R. 498 (C.A.) 575, 576, 597
Aro Co. Ltd, Re [1980] Ch. 196; [1980] 1 All E.R. 1067 .... 321, 375, 416, 430
Arochem v. Wilomi, 962 F.2d 496 (1992) (USA) 601
Arosa Kulm, The (No. 2) [1960] 1 Lloyd's Rep. 97 .... 36, 568

Arosa Star, The [1959] 2 Lloyd's Rep. 396 .... 36, 568
Arraiz, The (1924) 19 Ll.L.Rep. 235 .... 221, 222
Arum, The [1921] P. 12 589
Arzpeta, The (1921) 15 Asp. M.L.C. 426 568
Ashtiani v. Kashi [1986] 2 All E.R. 970 353
Aspen Trader, The [1981] 1 Lloyd's Rep. 273 289
Assunzione, The [1954] P. 150 .... 575, 578
Astro Vencedor Compania v. Mabanaft GmbH [1971] 2 Q.B. 588 337
Athena, The (1921) 8 Ll.L.Rep. 482 503
Athenic, The (1932) 42 Ll.L.Rep. 7 499
Athol, The (1842) 1 W. Rob. 374 260
Atlantic Emperor, The (No. 1) [1989] 1 Lloyd's Rep. 554 566
Atlantic Emperor, The (No. 2). See Marc Rich and Co. AG v. Societa Italiana Impianti PA.
Atlantic Song, The [1983] 2 Lloyd's Rep. 394 247
Atlantic Span, The, 1987 ETL 40 (Rechtbank van Koophandel Antwerp) 113
Atlantic Star, The [1974] A.C. 436 .... 250, 251
Atlas, The (1827) 2 Hag. Adm. 48 41
Atlas Pride, The [1994] LMLN 388 (High Ct. Singapore) 291, 324
Attika Hope, The [1988] 1 Lloyd's Rep. 439 .... 466, 505
Attock Cement Co. Ltd v. Romanian Bank for Foreign Trade [1989] 1 Lloyd's Rep. 572 575
Attorney General of New Zealand v. Ortiz and Others [1982] 1 Lloyd's Rep. 173; [1982] 2 Lloyd's Rep.
   224 (C.A.) 562
August 8th, The [1983] 1 Lloyd's Rep. 351 211
August Leonhardt, The [1984] 1 Lloyd's Rep. 322 214
Australian Commercial Research and Development Ltd v. ANZ Bank Ltd [1989] 3 All E.R. 65 250
Avant Petroleum Inc. v. Gatoil Overseas Inc. [1986] 2 Lloyd's Rep. 236 359
Aveling Barford, Re [1988] 3 All E.R. 1019 444
Aventicum, The [1978] 1 Lloyd's Rep. 184 199

BVT v. General Accident (1977) ECD 1–8–B1 239
Babcock v. Jackson, 240 N.Y.S. 2d 743 (1963); [1963] 2 Lloyd's Rep. 286 590
Baccus SRL v. Services National del Trigo [1957] 1 Q.B. 438 256
Bain Clarkson v. Owners of the Ship "Sea Friends" [1991] 2 Lloyd's Rep. 322 (C.A.) 71
Baiona, The [1992] 2 Lloyd's Rep. 121; [1992] 1 All E.R. 346 289
Baleares, The [1991] 2 Lloyd's Rep. 318; [1991] 3 All E.R. 554 285
Balkanbank v. Taher [1994] 4 All E.R. 239; [1995] 2 All E.R. 904 (C.A.) 305, 356
Banco Atlantico SA v. British Bank of the Middle East [1990] 2 Lloyd's Rep. 504 ..... 251, 253
Bank Mellat v. Kazmi [1989] 1 All E.R. 925 (C.A.) 361
Bank of Baroda v. Vysya Bank Ltd [1994] 2 Lloyd's Rep. 87 .... 565, 575, 587
Bank of Credit and Commerce (Hong Kong) Ltd v. Sonali Bank [1995] 1 Lloyd's Rep. 227 250
Bank of Credit and Commerce International, Re (No. 9) [1994] 3 All E.R. 764 (C.A.) 357
Bank of Crete SA v. Koskotas [1991] 2 Lloyd's Rep. 587 (C.A.) 361
Bank of Scotland v. Seitz, 1990 SLT 584; [1991] I.L.Pr. 426 (Court of Session) 145, 151, 162
Bankers Trust v. Galadari [1986] 3 All E.R. 794 (C.A.) 557
Barber v. Lamb (1860) 8 C.B. (N.S.) 95 617
Barclay-Johnson v. Yuill [1980] 1 W.L.R. 1259 .... 352, 359
Barclays Bank v. Hahn [1989] 1 All E.R. 723 176
Barclays Bank v. Rosenberg [1985] LMLN 147 356
Barclays Bank plc v. Glasgow City Council [1994] 4 All E.R. 865 (C.A.) 157, 162, 165, 166, 595
Barenbels, The [1984] 2 Lloyd's Rep. 388 .... 26, 336, 388, 462
Barnato, Re [1949] Ch. 258 553
Barton Henderson v. Merritt [1993] 1 Lloyd's Rep. 540 268
Bass Reefer, The [1992] LMLN 335 67
Bassini v. Santor [1986] ELD 354 113
Basso Legnami SpA v. The Licenses Insurance Co. and Others, ECD 1–17.1.2.–B7 (Trib. di
   Genova) 112, 115
Baumwool Manufactur v. Furness [1893] A.C. 8 405
Bayer AG v. Winter [1986] 1 All E.R. 733 (C.A.) 361
Baytur v. Finagro [1992] Lloyd's Rep. 134 275
Bazias 3 and 4, The [1993] 1 Lloyd's Rep. 101 .... 5, 302, 330, 331, 335, 338, 342
Beckham v. Drake (1849) 2 H.L. Cas. 579 411
Bee, The (1822) 2 Dods. 498 .... 44, 67

Behnke v. Bede Shipping Co. [1927] 1 K.B. 649 ....479, 552
Bekhor & Co. v. Bilton [1981] Q.B. 923; [1981] 1 Lloyd's Rep. 491 (C.A.) 347, 360, 361
Beldis, The [1936] P. 51 (C.A.) 63, 64, 291, 380, 430
Belgian Default Judgment, Re a [1992] I.L.Pr. 528 (Fed. Sup. Ct. Germany) 639, 641
Benarty, The [1985] Q.B. 325; [1984] 2 Lloyd's Rep. 244 (C.A.); reversing [1983] 2 Lloyd's Rep.
  50 ....131, 245, 247, 519, 565
Beneficial Finance Corpn. Ltd v. Price [1965] 1 Lloyd's Rep. 556   46
Berghoefer (F.) GmbH KG v. ASA (221/84) [1986] 2 CMLR 13 (ECJ)   112
Berisford Plc v. New Hampshire Insurance Co. [1990] 2 Q.B. 631; [1990] 1 Lloyd's Rep. 454; [1990]
  2 All E.R. 321 ....117, 141, 242
Berkeley Administration Inc. v. McLelland [1990] 1 All E.R. 958 (C.A.) 301, 309, 646
Berny, The [1979] Q.B. 80; [1977] 2 Lloyd's Rep. 533; [1978] 1 All E.R. 1068 ....197, 207
Berostar, The [1970] 2 Lloyd's Rep. 402   411
Bertie, The (1886) 6 Asp. M.L.C. 26   263
Beta, The (1869) L.R. 2 P.C. 447   33
Betty Ott, The [1992] 1 NZLR 655 (C.A. New Zealand) 491, 492, 564
Bineta, The [1967] 1 W.L.R. 121   45
Birchglen, The [1990] 3 F.C. 301 (Canada) 412, 415
Birkett v. James [1978] A.C. 297; [1977] 2 All E.R. 801 (H.L.) 227, 228
Bishopgate Finance v. Homan, The Times, 14 July 1994   459
Black v. Williams [1895] 1 Ch. 408 ....489, 490
Black v. Yates [1991] 1 Lloyd's Rep. 181   607
Black Clawson International Ltd v. Papierwerke Waldof-Aschaffenburg AG [1981] 2 Lloyd's Rep.
  446 ....279, 580
Blanche, The (1887) 6 Asp. M.L.C. 272   482
Blankaert and Willems PVBA v. Trost (139/80) [1981] ECR 819; [1982] 2 CMLR 1 (ECJ)   154
Blankenstein, The [1983] 3 All E.R. 510   553
Blitz, The [1992] 2 Lloyd's Rep. 441 ....346, 454, 473, 491, 497, 508
Blohn v. Desser [1962] 2 Q.B. 116   615
Blue Wave, The [1982] 1 Lloyd's Rep. 151 ....216, 248
Bock v. Gorrissen (1861) 30 L.J. Ch. 39   447
Bold Buccleugh, The (1851) 7 Moo. P.C. 267 (P.C.) 25, 28, 32, 33, 35, 226, 380, 381, 389–393, 400, 402
Boleslaw Chrobry, The [1974] 2 Lloyd's Rep. 308   594
Bonacina, Re [1912] 2 Ch. 394   576
Bonapart, The (1853) 8 Moo. P.C. 459   407
Bonaparte, The (1859) 7 Not. Cas. Supp. 55   41
Bond Worth Ltd, Re [1980] Ch. 228 ....471, 475
Bondy v. Lloyd's Bank, The Times, 13 March 1991   173
Boocock v. Hilton International Co. [1993] 4 All E.R. 19 (C.A.) 176, 179, 227
Booth Steamship Co. Ltd v. Cargo Fleet Iron Ltd [1916] 2 K.B. 570   497
Borag, The [1981] 1 Lloyd's Rep. 483   338
Boral Gas, The [1988] 1 Lloyd's Rep. 342   462
Borden (UK) Ltd v. Scottish Timber Products Ltd [1981] Ch. 25 ....459, 475, 552
Bosma Meubel Impex BV v. Hacker Gerechsthof Leeuwarden [1991] I.L.Pr. 384   150
Bosworth, The (No. 3) [1962] 1 Lloyd's Rep. 483   30
Boucraa, The [1994] 1 A.C. 486; [1994] 1 Lloyd's Rep. 251; [1994] 1 All E.R. 20 (H.L.) 281, 290
Bovenkerk, The [1973] 1 Lloyd's Rep. 63   594
Bowbelle, The [1990] 1 Lloyd's Rep. 532; [1990] 3 All E.R. 476 ....325, 340, 529, 535
Bowes, Re (1886) 33 Ch. D. 586   447
Bowmaker Ltd v. Wycombe Motors Ltd [1946] K.B. 505 ....447, 497
Boys v. Chaplin [1971] A.C. 356 (H.L.) 569, 572, 589–591
Bradley v. Newsom [1919] A.C. 16   399
Bragg v. Oceanus Mutual Underwriting Association (Bermuda) Ltd [1982] 2 Lloyd's Rep. 132   267
Bramarand, The (1968) unreported (Fo. 265)   415
Brandao v. Barnett (1846) 3 C.B. 519   447
Brazendale & Co. Ltd v. Saint Freres SA [1970] 2 Lloyd's Rep. 34   622
Bremen, The and Another, v. Zapata Off-Shore Co. [1972] 2 Lloyd's Rep. 315; 407 U.S. 1 (1972)   245
Bremer Oeltransport GmbH v. Drewry [1933] 1 K.B. 753 ....64, 291
Bremer Vulkan Schiffbau und Maschinenfabrik v. South India Shipping Corpn. [1981] A.C. 909; [1981]
  1 Lloyd's Rep. 253 (H.L.) 282, 290
Brenner v. Reynolds (318/93) [1995] All E.R. (E.C.) 278; [1994] I.L.Pr. 720 (ECJ) 117, 144
Brennero SAS v. Wendel GmbH (258/83) [1986] 1 CMLR 59 (ECJ) 644, 650

Breydon Merchant, The [1992] 1 Lloyd's Rep. 373 529
Brightlife Ltd, Re [1986] 3 All E.R. 673 456
Bristol Airport plc v. Powdrill [1990] Ch. 744; [1990] 2 All E.R. 493 (C.A.) 442, 454
British Aerospace plc v. Dee Howard Co. [1993] 1 Lloyd's Rep. 368 .... 242, 252, 255
British Airport plc v. Powdrill [1990] 2 All E.R. 493 376
British Airways Board v. Laker Airways [1984] 3 All E.R. 39 (H.L.) 271
British Trade, The [1924] P. 104 .... 35, 36
Broadmayne, The [1916] P. 64 261
Brodin v. Seljan, 1973 S.C. 213 .... 574, 577, 588
Brokaw v. Seatrain UK Ltd [1971] 2 Q.B. 476 562
Broken Hill Proprietary Co. Ltd v. Theodore Xenakis [1982] 2 Lloyd's Rep. 304 .... 174, 190
Brond v. Broomhall [1906] 1 K.B. 571 .... 46, 47
Brown v. Thornton (1837) 6 A. & E. 185 573
Brownton Ltd v. Edward Moore Inbucon Ltd [1985] 3 All E.R. 499 (C.A.) 408, 493
Brunton v. Electrical Engineering Corpn. [1892] 1 Ch. 434 .... 486, 495
Bulgaria, The [1964] 2 Lloyd's Rep. 543 342
Bulk Oil (Zug) AG v. Sun International Ltd and Another [1983] 1 Lloyd's Rep. 655; [1983] 2 Lloyd's
    Rep. 587 (C.A.) 286
Burgis v. Constantine [1908] 2 K.B. 484 .... 489, 491
Burns, The [1907] P. 137 (C.A.) 383, 555
Burston Finance v. Speirway [1974] 1 W.L.R. 1648 .... 373, 443
Byzantion, The (1922) 12 Ll.L.Rep. 9 .... 336, 500

CBS UK Ltd v. Lambert [1982] 3 All E.R. 237 360
CFEM Facades SA v. Boris Construction Ltd [1992] I.L.Pr. 561 304
CILFIT Srl v. Ministry of Health [1982] ECR 3415; [1983] 1 CMLR 472 (ECJ) 88
CT Bowring (Insurance) Ltd v. Corsi Partners Ltd [1994] 2 Lloyd's Rep. 567 (C.A.) ... 301, 302, 356
Cahill v. Dawson (1857) 3 C.B. (N.S.) 106 .... 445, 452
Cala Cristal SA v. Emran Al-Borno, The Times, 6 May 1994; [1994] LMLN 383 .... 359, 360
Caltex Oil (Australia) Pty Ltd v. The Dredge Willemstad (1975–76) 136 C.L.R. 529 .... 52, 210
Campbell v. Van Aart [1993] I.L.Pr. 314 (High Ct. Ireland) 148, 150
Campbell International Trading House v. Van Aart [1993] I.L.Pr. 314 108
Campbell Mussels v. Thompson (1984) Law. Soc. Gaz. 2140 360
Canada Enterprises Corpn. Ltd v. MacNab Distilleries Ltd [1981] Com.L.R. 167 .... 200, 557
Canadian National SS Co. v. Watson [1959] 1 D.L.R. 273 (Canada) 589
Candy SpA v. Schell, 1979 ECD 1–5.3–B11 152
Cannon Screen Entertainments Ltd v. Handmade Films Ltd, 11 July 1989 (unreported) 242
Cap Bon, The [1967] 1 Lloyd's Rep. 543 284
Capelloni v. Pelkmans (119/84) [1985] ECR 3147; [1986] 1 CMLR 388 (ECJ) 644, 649
Capital Finance Co. Ltd v. Stokes [1969] Ch. 261 486
Capitan San Luis, The [1993] 2 Lloyd's Rep. 573 .... 5, 530
Cargo Ex Galam (1863) 2 Moo. P.C. (N.S.) 216 504
Cargo Ex Schiller, The (1877) 2 P.D. 145 .... 28, 29, 395
Cargo Ex Sultan, The (1859) Swab. 504 .... 23, 41
Carmania II, The [1963] 2 Lloyd's Rep. 152 67
Carrick v. Hancock (1895) 12 T.L.R. 59 615
Carron v. Federal Republic of Germany (198/85) [1987] 1 CMLR 838 (ECJ) 645
Carrow Towing Co. v. The Ed McWilliams (1919) 46 D.L.R. 506 44
Case No. 9 U 167/75 ECD 1–16.5–B2 107
Casper Trader, The [1992] 3 All E.R. 132 (C.A.) 175
Cassils and Sassoon v. Holdenwood Bleaching Co. Ltd (1914) 84 L.J.K.B. 834 445
Castanho v. Brown and Root (UK) [1981] A.C. 557 .... 268, 269
Castle Alpha, The [1989] 2 Lloyd's Rep. 383 288
Castlegate, The [1893] A.C. 38 (H.L.) 39, 40, 397, 398, 403, 405, 406, 410
Castrique v. Imrie (1870) L.R. 4 H.L. 414 .... 613, 617
Cavendish, The [1993] 2 Lloyd's Rep. 292 402
Cayne v. Global Natural Resources plc [1984] 1 All E.R. 225 297
Cebu, The (No. 1) [1983] 1 Lloyd's Rep. 302 465–467
Cebu, The (No. 2) [1990] 2 Lloyd's Rep. 316 .... 462, 466, 467
Celtic King, The [1894] P. 175 482
Cerro Colorado, The [1993] 1 Lloyd's Rep. 58 .... 335, 417, 507, 555
Chalmers v. Pardoe [1963] 3 All E.R. 552 458

Champion, The [1934] P. 1 395
Channel Tunnel Group Ltd v. Balfour Beatty Construction Ltd [1992] 2 Lloyd's Rep. 7 (C.A.); [1993]
   A.C. 334; [1993] 1 Lloyd's Rep. 291; [1993] 1 All E.R. 664 (H.L.) 185, 283, 303, 349, 350, 564
Chappell v. Cooper [1980] 2 All E.R. 463 (C.A.) 223
Charger, The [1966] 1 Lloyd's Rep. 670; [1966] 3 All E.R. 117 .... 346, 453, 473, 506, 508
Charlotte, The [1920] P. 78 342
Charman v. WOC Offshore BV [1993] 2 Lloyd's Rep. 551 .... 139, 142, 236
Chartered Bank v. Daklouche [1980] 1 All E.R. 205 352
Chartered Mercantile Bank of India v. Netherlands India Navigation Co. (1883) 10 Q.B. 521 .... 575, 589
Chase Manhattan Bank v. Israel British Bank [1979] 3 All E.R. 1025 596
Chellaram & Sons (London) Ltd v. Butlers Warehousing & Distribution Ltd [1978] 2 Lloyd's Rep.
   412 ....441, 444, 445
Cheltenham and Gloucester Building Society v. Ricketts [1994] 3 All E.R. 276 .... 355, 356
Cheshire Witch, The (1864) B. & L. 362 338
Chieftain, The (1863) B. & L. 104 .... 40, 417
Chimera, The (1852) 11 L.T. 113 502
Choice Investments Ltd v. Jeromninon [1981] 1 All E.R. 225 557
Choko Star, The [1995] LMLN 411 225
Chr Knudsen, The [1932] P. 153 32
Christiansborg, The (1885) 10 P.D. 141 ....332, 413, 415
Chrysovolandou Dyo, The [1981] 1 Lloyd's Rep. 159 465
City of Mecca, The (1881) 6 P.D. 106; reversing on the facts (1879) 5 P.D. 28 ....23, 342, 613, 618
Clan Grant, The (1887) 6 Asp. M.L.C. 144 44
Clara, The (1855) Swab. 1 342
Clark v. Bowring, 1908 S.C. 1168 411
Clay v. Sudgrave (1700) 1 Salk. 33 .... 381, 406
Cleon, The [1983] 1 Lloyd's Rep. 586 (C.A.) 280
Cleveland Museum of Art v. Capricorn Art International SA [1990] 2 Lloyd's Rep. 166 252
Clifford Chance v. Owners of the Vessel Atlantic Trader 71
Clifford Maersk, The [1982] 2 Lloyd's Rep. 251 214
Clothing Sales Contract, Re a [1995] I.L.Pr. 72 (Oberlandsgericht Munchen) 236
Clough Mill Ltd v. Martin [1984] 1 All E.R. 721; [1984] 3 All E.R. 982 (C.A.) 471, 475, 486
Clupea, The [1982] LMLN 62 (Court of Session) 453
Clydesdale Bank v. Walker and Bain, 1926 S.C. 72 411
Coast Lines Ltd v. Hudig & Veder Chartering NV [1972] 1 Q.B. 34 .... 575, 578
Cocona Energy, The, 1977 folio No. 174, cited in Bain Clarkson v. Owners of the Ship "Sea Friends"
   [1991] 2 Lloyd's Rep. 322 (C.A.) 71
Cohn, Re [1945] 1 Ch. 5 574
Coignet SA v. Banca Commerciale Italiana [1992] I.L.Pr. 450 116
Coker, Ex parte (1875) L.R. 10 Ch. App. 652 321
Colorado, The [1923] P. 102 571
Comdel Commodities Ltd v. Siporex Trade SA [1990] 2 All E.R. 552 (H.L.) 288, 289
Comet, The [1965] 1 Lloyd's Rep. 195 40
Commercial Bank of the Near East plc v. ABC and D [1989] 2 Lloyd's Rep. 319 358
Comoco v. M/V El Centro Americano [1984] AMC 1434 568
Compagnie d'Armement Maritime SA v. Compagnie Tunisienne de Navigation SA [1971] A.C. 572 .. 277,
   575, 578, 580
Company A v. Republic of X [1990] 2 Lloyd's Rep. 520 ....257, 258
Conet, The [1965] 1 Lloyd's Rep. 195 473
Conoco Britannia, The [1972] 2 Q.B. 543 ....51, 61, 63, 67, 177, 195, 351, 550, 556
Constables Case (1610) 5 Co. Rep. 106a 399
Constancia, The (1846) 2 W. Rob. 460 474
Constellation, The [1965] 2 Lloyd's Rep. 538 321
Continental Bank NA v. Aeakos Compania Naviera SA [1994] 1 Lloyd's Rep. 505 (C.A.) 111, 233, 242,
   269, 270, 549
Coppée Lavalin SA v. Ken Ren Chemicals and Fertilisers Ltd [1994] 2 Lloyd's Rep. 109; [1994] 2 All
   E.R. 449 (H.L.) 274, 282, 283, 303
Coral Rose, The [1991] 1 Lloyd's Rep. 563 200
Coral Rose, The (No. 3) [1991] 2 Lloyd's Rep. 374 ....200, 360
Coreck v. Sevrybokholodflot, 1994 SLT 893 327
Corfu Navigation v. Mobil Shipping Co. [1991] 2 Lloyd's Rep. 52 301
Cornelia Henrietta, The (1866) L.R. 1 A. & E. 51 411

Cornhill Insurance plc v. Barclay [1992] LMLN 340 355
Corser v. Husely (1688) Comb. 135 381
Costellow v. Somerset County Council [1993] 1 All E.R. 952 228
Countess, The [1923] A.C. 345 509
County and District Properties v. Lyell [1991] 1 W.L.R. 653 (C.A.) 228
Coupland v. Arabian Gulf Petroleum Co. [1983] 2 All E.R. 434; [1983] 3 All E.R. 226 (C.A.) 572,
574, 590
Courageous Colocotronis, The [1979] W.A.R. 19 47
Craighall, The [1910] P. 207 395
Crathie, The [1897] P. 178 535
Cretan Harmony, The [1978] 1 Lloyd's Rep. 425; [1978] 3 All E.R. 164 .... 494, 498
Cretanor Maritime Co. Ltd v. Irish Management Ltd [1978] 1 Lloyd's Rep. 425 347
Cristina, The [1938] A.C. 485 256
Crusader, The [1907] P. 15 27
Cumming v. Scottish Daily Record and Others, The Times, 8 June 1995 167
Currie v. M'Knight [1897] A.C. 97 ....28, 32, 56, 428
Curtis v. Wild [1991] 4 All E.R. 172 27
Custom Made Commercial Ltd v. Stawa Metallbau GmbH [1993] I.L.Pr. 490 (Bundesgerichtshof);
[1994] I.L.Pr. 516 (ECJ) 109, 149, 150
Customs and Excise Commissioners v. Air Canada [1991] 2 Q.B. 446 (C.A.) 49
Cybele, The (1878) 3 P.D. 8 263

DSQ Property Co. Ltd v. Lotus Cars Ltd [1987] 1 W.L.R. 127 301
Dagmara and Ama Antxine, The [1988] 1 Lloyd's Rep. 431 32
Daien Maru No. 18, The [1986] 1 Lloyd's Rep. 387 (Singapore) 51, 194, 309
D'Almeida Araujo Lda. v. Becker & Co. [1953] 2 Q.B. 329 572
Dalmia Cement v. National Bank of Pakistan [1975] Q.B. 9 621
Damavand, The [1993] LMLN 357 (C.A. Singapore) 207, 322
Dante, The (1846) 2 W. Rob. 427 41
Danvaern Production A/S v. Schuhfabrik Otterbeck GmbH [1995] I.L.Pr. 649 158
Daring, The (1868) L.R. 2 A. & E. 260 502
Davenport v. Corinthian Motor Policies at Lloyd's, 1991 SLT 774 .... 151, 162
Davies (UK) Ltd v. Marc Rich and Co. Ltd [1985] 2 Lloyd's Rep. 423 (C.A.) 289
De Bloos Sprl v. Bouyer SA (14/76) [1976] ECR 1497; [1977] 1 CMLR 60 (ECJ) 148, 154, 238
De Bry v. Fitzgerald [1990] 1 All E.R. 560 308
De Dampierre v. De Dampierre [1988] A.C. 92 253
De Pina v. MS Birka [1994] I.L.Pr. 694 238
De Wolf v. Cox BV (42/76) [1976] ECR 1759; [1977] 2 CMLR 43 (ECJ) 231, 626
Dearle v. Hall (1823) 3 Russ. 1 493
Debaecker v. Bouwman (49/84) [1986] 2 CMLR 400 (ECJ) 639–641
Decision of the Landgericht, Hamburg, 24 April 1979, ECD 1–1.2–B12 92
Deerness v. John R. Keeble & Son (Brantham) Ltd [1983] 2 Lloyd's Rep. 260 223
Deichland, The [1990] 1 Q.B. 361; [1989] 2 Lloyd's Rep. 113; [1989] 2 All E.R. 1066 (C.A.) 94, 120,
127, 206, 237, 307, 382, 383, 404, 627
Denby v. Hellenic Mediterranean Lines [1994] 1 Lloyd's Rep. 320 242
Denilauler v. SNC Couchet Freres (125/79) [1980] ECR 1553 [1981] 1 CMLR 62 (ECJ) 304, 628
Dennis and Sons v. Cork Steamship Co. Ltd [1913] 2 K.B. 393 450
Derby v. Weldon (No. 1) [1989] 1 All E.R. 469 353
Derby v. Weldon (No. 2) [1989] 1 All E.R. 1002 (C.A.) 304, 347, 353, 359, 361, 362, 549, 557
Derby v. Weldon (No. 6) [1990] 3 All E.R. 263 ....354, 361
Derbyshire, The [1988] A.C. 276; [1988] 1 Lloyd's Rep. 109 (H.L.) 55
Despina G.K., The [1983] Q.B. 214; [1982] 2 Lloyd's Rep. 555 .... 21, 23, 210, 309, 324, 432, 614, 618
Despina Pontikos, The [1975] E.A.R. 38 (C.A. East Africa) 200, 479
Despina R, The [1979] A.C. 685; [1979] 1 Lloyd's Rep. 1 (H.L.) 551
Deutsche Genossenschaftsbank v. Brasserie du Pecheur (148/84) [1986] 2 CMLR 496 (ECJ) 626, 644, 650
Devon, The (1923) 16 Asp. M.L.C. 268 51
Dictator, The [1892] P. 64, 304 ....177, 344, 380, 382, 555
Dimbleby and Sons Ltd v. NUJ [1984] 1 All E.R. 751 (H.L.) 297
Diplock, Re [1948] Ch. 465 (C.A.); affirmed [1951] A.C. 251 459
Disperser, The [1920] P. 228 222
Ditta Estascis Sulotti v. RUWA GmbH (24/76) [1976] ECR 1831; [1977] 1 CMLR 345 (ECJ) 111
Dong Wha Enterprise Co. Ltd v. Crownson Shipping Ltd [1995] 1 Lloyd's Rep. 113 ....174, 181

Dowthorpe, The (1843) 2 W. Rob. 73 ....41, 398, 399
Dresser UK Ltd v. Falcongate Freight Management Ltd [1991] 2 Lloyd's Rep. 557 (C.A.) 115, 234, 235,
239, 241, 305, 517, 537
Druid, The (1842) 2 W. Rob. 391 404
Du Pont v. Agnew [1987] 2 Lloyd's Rep. 585 251
Duijnstee v. Lodewijk Goderbaver (288/82) [1983] ECR 3663; [1985] 1 CMLR 220 (ECJ) 98, 99
Dunbee Ltd v. Gilman & Co. (Australia) Pty. [1968] 2 Lloyd's Rep. 394 (NSW) 581
Durbeck v. Arco International Transport BV, 1985 ECD 321 133

EMI Records v. Modern Music [1992] 1 All E.R. 616 628
Eagle, The [1977] 2 Lloyd's Rep. 70 55
Eagle Star Insurance Ltd v. Yuval Insurance Ltd [1978] 1 Lloyd's Rep. 357 189
Edward Oliver, The (1867) L.R. 1 A. & E. 379 503
Edwin, The (1864) B. & L. 281 407
Effer SpA v. Kantner (38/81) [1982] ECR 825; [1984] 2 CMLR 667 (ECR) 147
El Ajou v. Dollar Land Holdings plc [1993] 3 All E.R. 717 596
El Amria, The [1981] 2 Lloyd's Rep. 119 (C.A.) 246, 247, 579
El Amria and El Minia, The [1982] 2 Lloyd's Rep. 28 (C.A.) 576
Eleanora Charlotta, The (1823) 1 Hag. Adm. 156 28
Electric Supply Stores v. Gaywood (1909) 100 L.T. 855 ....446, 497
Elefanten Schuh GmbH v. Pierre Jacqmain (150/80) [1981] ECR 1671; [1982] 3 CMLR 1 (ECJ) 107,
108, 110, 114, 116
Eleftheria, The [1970] P. 94 ....246, 247
Eleftherios, The [1982] 1 Lloyd's Rep. 351 ....353, 357, 363
Elin, The (1882) 8 P.D. 39 ....474, 502, 503
Eliza, The (1833) 3 Hag. Adm. 87 67
Ella A. Clarke, The (1863) B. & L. 32 390
Ellerine Bros. (Pty) Ltd v. Klinger [1982] 2 All E.R. 737 280
Elli 2, The [1985] 1 Lloyd's Rep. 107 279
Elmville, The (No. 2) [1904] P. 422 ....39, 40
Elton, The [1891] P. 265 390
Elwyn (Cottons) Ltd v. Pearle Designs Ltd [1990] I.L.Pr. 40 303
Emmanuel Colocotronis, The (No. 1) [1982] 1 Lloyd's Rep. 297 286
Emre II, The [1989] 2 Lloyd's Rep. 182 ....330, 340
Energie, The (1875) L.R. 6 P.C. 306 ....450, 452
Enforcement of a Foreign Costs Order, Re the [1986] ECC 481 (Oberlandsgericht Frankfurt) 627
Enforcement of a French Sequestration Order, Re [1979] ECC 321 636
Engdiv Ltd v. Trentham Ltd, 1990 SLT 617 ....147, 162
English Judgment, Re an [1993] I.L.Pr. 653 (Oberlandsgericht Hamm) 634, 638, 641
Epimenidis, The [1986] LMLN 186 (C.A. Ghent) 603
Esal v. Pujara [1989] 2 Lloyd's Rep. 479 (C.A.) 177, 189
Eskbridge, The [1931] P. 51 505
Esso Brussels, The [1973] 2 Lloyd's Rep. 73 (C.A.) 594
Esso Malaysia, The [1975] Q.B. 198; [1974] 2 Lloyd's Rep. 143; [1974] 2 All E.R. 705 ....55, 564, 592
Etablissement Esefka International Anstalt v. Central Bank of Nigeria [1979] 1 Lloyd's Rep. 445
(C.A.) 359
Etri Fans v. NMB (UK) Ltd [1987] 2 All E.R. 763 280
Europa, The (1863) 2 Moo. N.S. 1 226
European Asian Bank AG v. Punjab and Sind Bank (No. 2) [1983] 1 W.L.R. 642 (C.A.) 177
Eurostar, The [1993] 1 Lloyd's Rep. 106 ....397, 435
Eurosun, The and the Eurostar [1993] 1 Lloyd's Rep. 106 554
Eurotrader, The [1987] 1 Lloyd's Rep. 418 289
Eva, The [1921] P. 454 474
Evangelismos, The (1858) Swab. 378 337
Evans Construction Co. Ltd v. Charrington & Co. Ltd [1983] 1 All E.R. 310 225
Evelyn, Re [1894] 2 Q.B. 302 ....321, 376, 416
Evia Luck, The [1992] 1 Lloyd's Rep. 115 (H.L.) 577
Evimeria, The [1982] 1 Lloyd's Rep. 55 286
Evpo Agnic, The [1988] 2 Lloyd's Rep. 411; [1988] 3 All E.R. 810 (C.A.) 198, 200, 203
Excess Insurance Co. Ltd v. Astra SA Insurance Co. [1995] LMLN 396 184
Exchange Control and a Greek Guarantor, Re [1993] I.L.Pr. 298 ....112, 113
Exeter, The (1799) 1 C. Rob. 173 504

Exhill Coal Mining Co., Re (1864) 4 De G.J. & Sm. 377 375

Fairfield Shipbuilders & Engineering Co. Ltd v. Gardner, Mountain & Co. Ltd (1911) 104 L.T.
   288 452
Fairfold Properties Ltd v. Exmouth Dock Co. Ltd (No. 2) [1992] 4 All E.R. 289 496
Fairport, The (1882) 8 P.D. 48 ....39, 40, 226
Fairport, The (1965) 2 Lloyd's Rep. 183 ....36, 37, 335, 554, 567
Fairport, The (No. 3) [1966] 2 Lloyd's Rep. 253 36
Fairport, The (No. 5) [1967] 2 Lloyd's Rep. 162 67
Faith, The [1993] 2 Lloyd's Rep. 408 285
Fakih v. A. P. Moller Ltd [1994] 1 Lloyd's Rep. 103 ....268, 270
Falcon, The [1977] 2 Lloyd's Rep. 243 473
Falcon, The [1981] 1 Lloyd's Rep. 13 ....334, 335
Falstria, The [1988] 1 Lloyd's Rep. 495 ....253, 534, 535, 537
Fanchon, The (1880) 5 P.D. 173 482
Far Eastern Shipping Co. v. AKP Sovcomflot [1995] 1 Lloyd's Rep. 520 ....275, 623
Father Thames, The [1979] 2 Lloyd's Rep. 364 ....33, 197, 201, 403, 405
Fehmarn, The [1957] 2 Lloyd's Rep. 551 247
Felixstowe Dock & Railway Co. and Others v. United States Lines Inc. [1987] 2 Lloyd's Rep. 76; [1988]
   2 All E.R. 77 354
Feronia, The (1868) L.R. 2 A. & E. 65 ....39, 40
Ferret, The (1883) 8 App. Cas. 329 407
Fierbinti, The [1994] LMLN 396 ....208, 323
Finnish Marine Insurance Co. Ltd v. Protective National Co. [1989] 2 Lloyd's Rep. 99; [1989] 2 All E.R.
   929 ....148, 184, 190
Finnrose, The [1994] 1 Lloyd's Rep. 559 ....220, 228
Firma Mund and Fester v. Firma Hatrex International Transport (398/92) [1994] I.L.Pr. 264 (ECJ) 309,
   626, 646
Firma P v. Firma K (178/83) [1985] 2 CMLR 271 (ECJ) 651
Fisher v. Smith (1878) 4 App. Cas. 1 443
Flora, The (1886) L.R. 1 A. & E. 45 ....322, 414
Foreign Exchange Rates, Re [1994] I.L.Pr. 703 636
Fort Kipp, The [1985] 2 Lloyd's Rep. 168 ....449, 462
Fort Laramie, The (1922) 31 C.L.R. 56 199
Forward v. West Sussex C.C. [1995] 4 All E.R. 207 175
Foxcraft v. Wood (1828) 4 Russ. 487 447
Foxe v. Scotsman Publications Ltd, 1994 TLR 84 167
Frances, The (1820) 2 Dods. 420 46
Francesco Nullo, The [1973] 1 Lloyd's Rep. 72 594
Frank Pais, The [1986] 1 Lloyd's Rep. 529 240
Freccia Del Nord, The [1989] 1 Lloyd's Rep. 388 235
Freedom, The (1871) 1 Asp. M.L.C. 136 324
Freightline One, The [1986] 1 Lloyd's Rep. 266 ....346, 453, 454, 473, 509
Freir, The, The Albert (1875) 2 Asp. M.L.C. 589 324
Frotanorte, The [1995] 2 Lloyd's Rep. 254 290
Fulham, The [1898] P. 206; affirmed [1899] P. 251 (C.A.) 31, 451
Fusilier, The (1865) 3 Moo. P.C. (N.S.) 51 (P.C.) 28, 29

Gaetano and Maria, The (1882) 7 P.D. 137 573
Galaxias, The [1989] 1 Can. Fed. 386 601
Galaxias, The [1989] IEC 386 474
Galerier Segovra Sprl v. Bonakdarian (25/76) [1976] ECR 1851; [1977] 1 CMLR 361 (ECJ) 111
Ganges, The (1869) L.R. 2 A. & E. 370 410
Gannon v. Band I Steam Packet Ltd [1994] I.L.Pr. 405 (Sup. Ct. Ireland) 157
Gapp v. Bond (1887) 19 Q.B.D. 200 479
Gardner v. Lachlan (1838) 4 Myl. & Cr. 129 493
Gas Float Whitton, The (No. 2) [1897] A.C. 337 ....395, 398
Gascoigne v. Pyrah [1994] I.L.Pr. 82 (C.A.) 145
Gaupen, The (1925) 22 Ll.L.Rep. 57 497
Gay Toucan, The [1968] 2 Lloyd's Rep. 245 344
Gemma, The [1899] P. 285 344
Genel Maklyati SA v. Compagnie Générale Maritime SA (1982) 1983 ECD 144 634

General Palmer, The (1828) 2 Hag. Adm. 176 67
Geobra Brankstatten GmbH v. Big Spielwarenfabrik 1977, ECD 1–5.3–B5 (District Ct. Amsterdam) .. 152
George Barker (Transport) Ltd v. Eynon [1974] 1 Lloyd's Rep. 65; [1974] 1 All E.R. 900 .... 373, 441
George Gordon, The (1884) 9 P.D. 46 343
Gerling Konzern v. Amministrazione del Tesoro (201/82) [1983] ECR 2503; [1984] 3 CMLR 638
    (ECJ) 114, 141, 143
Giacinto Motta, The [1977] 2 Lloyd's Rep. 221 .... 521, 535, 537, 539
Gidrxslme Shipping v. Tantomar-Transportes [1994] 2 Lloyd's Rep. 392; [1994] 4 All E.R. 507 361
Gill and Duffus SA v. Ronda Futures [1994] 2 Lloyd's Rep. 67 373
Gina, The [1980] 1 Lloyd's Rep. 398 .... 61, 324, 337
Gladstone v. Birley (1817) 2 Mer. 401 455
Gladys, The [1988] 2 Lloyd's Rep. 221 (C.A.); [1990] 1 Lloyd's Rep. 297; [1990] 1 All E.R. 397
    (H.L.) 276, 279
Glasgow Navigation Co. v. Iron Ore Co. [1910] A.C. 293 267
Glegg v. Bromley [1912] 3 K.B. 474 409
Gobluchick, The (1840) 1 W. Rob. 143 266
Golaa, The [1926] P. 103 332
Goldean Mariner, The [1990] 2 Lloyd's Rep. 215 (C.A.) 174
Golden Anne, The [1984] 2 Lloyd's Rep. 489 270
Golden Elephant, The [1976] 2 Lloyd's Rep. 462 (C.A. Singapore) 338, 341
Golden Sands, The [1975] 2 Lloyd's Rep. 166 191
Golden Trader, The [1974] 1 Lloyd's Rep. 378 284
Good Herald, The [1987] 1 Lloyd's Rep. 236 211
Goring, The [1988] A.C. 831; [1988] 1 Lloyd's Rep. 397 (H.L.) 5, 28, 29, 31
Goulandris, The [1927] P. 182 417
Gourdain v. Nadler (133/78) [1979] ECR 733; [1979] 3 CMLR 180 (ECJ) 91, 627
Government of India v. Taylor [1955] A.C. 491 .... 562, 614
Government of the State of Kuwait v. Sir Frederick Snow & Partners [1981] 1 Lloyd's Rep. 656; [1983]
    1 Lloyd's Rep. 596 (C.A.); [1984] 1 Lloyd's Rep. 458 (H.L.) 274, 275, 622
Gracechurch v. Assicurazioni Generato [1994] I.L.Pr. 206 (Corte de Cassazione, Italy) 147
Gramlesraden plc v. Casa De Suecia SA [1994] 1 Lloyd's Rep. 433 233
Greenway and Barkers Case (1577) Godb. 260; 3 Black Book of Admiralty 103 381
Greenwood v. Bennett [1973] Q.B. 195 446
Gregos, The [1985] 2 Lloyd's Rep. 347 .... 439, 440
Grupo Torras SA v. Sheikh Al Sabah [1995] 1 Lloyd's Rep. 374; [1995] I.L.Pr. 667 (C.A.) 105, 175,
                                                                                              233, 235, 236, 238
Gubisch Maschinenfabrik KA v. Palumbo [1989] ECC 420 236
Gulf Bank KSC v. Mitsubishi Ltd [1994] 1 Lloyd's Rep. 323 184
Gulf Grain, The [1995] I.L.Pr. 600 147
Gulf Venture, The [1984] 2 Lloyd's Rep. 445 343
Gustaf, The (1862) Lush 506 .... 498, 501

Haabet, The [1899] P. 295 41
Hacker v. Euro Relais GmbH (280/90) [1992] I.L.Pr. 515 (ECJ) 104
Haeger and Schmidt GmbH v. Compagnie Francaise de Navigation, 2 March 1977, ECD 1–57–B4 (C.A.
    of Central Commission for Navigation of the Rhine) 136
Haiti (Republic of) v. Duvalier [1989] 1 Lloyd's Rep. 111; [1989] 1 All E.R. 456 (C.A.) 180, 306, 352
Halcyon Isle, The [1981] A.C. 221; [1980] 2 Lloyd's Rep. 325 (P.C.) 26, 29, 392, 393, 413, 489, 499,
                                                                               566, 568, 569, 571, 601, 602, 605, 615
Halcyon Skies, The [1977] Q.B. 14; [1976] 1 Lloyd's Rep. 461; [1976] 1 All E.R. 856 .... 26, 28, 35, 36,
                                                                                              407, 428, 435, 499
Halcyon the Great, The (No. 2) [1975] 1 Lloyd's Rep. 525 555
Halley, The (1868) L.R. 2 P.C. 193 589
Hamburg Star, The [1994] 1 Lloyd's Rep. 399 .... 59, 252, 254
Hanbridge Services Ltd v. Aerospace Communication Ltd [1993] I.L.Pr. 778 (Sup. Ct. Ireland) 151
Handelswekerij Gt Bier and Stichting Rein Water v. Mines de Potasse d'Alsace (21/76) [1976] ECR
    1735; [1977] 1 CMLR 284 (ECJ) 151
Handgate, The [1987] 1 Lloyd's Rep. 142 187
Handte GmbH v. TMCS (26/91) [1993] I.L.Pr. 5 (ECJ) 123, 147
Hannah Blumenthal, The [1983] 1 Lloyd's Rep. 103 290
Hantorex SpA v. SA Digital Research [1993] I.L.Pr. 501 (Cour d'Appel Paris) 110
Happy Pioneer, The [1983] HKLR 43 577

Harbour Assurance Co. (UK) Ltd v. Kansa General International Insurance Co. Ltd [1992] 1 Lloyd's Rep.
 81; [1993] 1 Lloyd's Rep. 455 (C.A.) 279
Harlow, The [1922] P. 175 395
Harmonie, The (1841) 1 W. Rob. 178 499
Harris v. Quine (1869) L.R. 4 Q.B. 653 ....570, 617
Harrods (Buenos Aires) Ltd, Re [1991] 4 All E.R. 334 (C.A.) 95, 233, 269
Hartford v. Jones (1698) 1 Ld. Ray. 393 451
Hassneh Insurance Co. v. Mew [1993] 2 Lloyd's Rep. 243 ....283, 553
Havhelt, The [1993] 1 Lloyd's Rep. 523 ....220, 247, 302
Hayter v. Nelson Insurance Co. [1990] 2 Lloyd's Rep. 265 280
Heather Bell, The [1901] P. 143 482
Heidberg, The [1994] 2 Lloyd's Rep. 287 ....93, 275, 277, 566, 576, 577, 579
Heinrich, The (1872) L.R. 3 A. & E. 505 ....496, 509
Heinrich Bjorn, The (1885) 10 P.D. 44 (C.A.); (1886) 11 App. Cas. 270 (H.L.) 26, 33, 43, 390, 428, 429
Helene Roth, The [1980] 1 Lloyd's Rep. 477; [1980] 1 All E.R. 1078 ....207, 208
Hendy Lennox Ltd v. Puttick Ltd [1984] 2 All E.R. 152 475
Henrik Sif, The [1982] 1 Lloyd's Rep. 456 ....214, 221
Hereward, The [1985] P. 284 46
Hero, The (1865) B. & L. 446 324
Hesperides Hotels Ltd v. Muftizade [1978] 2 All E.R. 1168 264
Hestia, The [1895] P. 193 28
Hill v. Wilson (1879) 4 C.P.D. 329 597
Hine Bros. v. The Steamship Syndicate Ltd (1895) 72 L.T. 79 452
Hingston v. Wendt (1876) 1 Q.B.D. 367 ....449, 451
Hiscox v. Outhwaite (No. 1) [1992] 1 A.C. 562; [1991] 2 Lloyd's Rep. 435; [1991] 3 All E.R. 641
 (H.L.) 278, 622
Hjemmet, The (1880) 5 P.D. 227 67
Hoegh Silvercrest, The [1962] 1 Lloyd's Rep. 9 51
Hoffman v. Kreig (145/86) [1987] ECR 645; [1990] I.L.Pr. 4 (ECJ) 629, 636, 642
Holderness v. Shackels (1824) 8 B. & C. 612 447
Holmes v. Bangladesh Biman Corpn. [1985] 1 All E.R. 852 (H.L.) 564
Honshu Gloria, The [1986] 2 Lloyd's Rep. 63 473
Hope, The (1840) 1 W. Rob. 154 382
Hope, The (1873) 1 Asp. M.L.C. 563 501–503
Horlock, The (1877) 2 P.D. 243 479
Hubbard v. Hamburger (20/90) The Times, 16 July 1993 (ECJ) 309
Huber v. Steiner (1835) 2 Bing. N.C. 202 570
Hughes v. Hughes [1958] P. 221 444
Hull No. 1, The and Hull No. 2 [1991] LMLN 310 474
Huth & Co. v. Lamport (1886) 16 Q.B.D. 735 451
Hutton v. Mofarrij [1989] 2 All E.R. 633 181

I Congreso del Partido, The [1978] Q.B. 500; [1980] 1 Lloyd's Rep. 23; [1978] 1 All E.R. 1169 (C.A.);
 [1981] 2 Lloyd's Rep. 367 (H.L.) 197, 199, 201, 259
ICI Fibres v. MAT Transport [1987] 1 F.L.R. 145 218
IP Metal Ltd v. Ruote Oz SpA [1993] 2 Lloyd's Rep. 60; affirmed [1992] 2 Lloyd's Rep. 560 ....110–112, 270
IP Metal Ltd v. Ruote Oz SpA (No. 2) [1994] 2 Lloyd's Rep. 560 233
ISC v. Guerin [1992] 2 Lloyd's Rep. 482 186
Ice Express, The [1990] I.L.Pr. 263 (District Ct. Livorno) 111
Igor, The [1956] 2 Lloyd's Rep. 271 507
Ile de Ceylan, The [1922] P. 256 509
Immacolata Conezione, The (1884) 9 P.D. 37 ....36, 473, 498
Import of Italian Sports Cars, Re [1992] I.L.Pr. 188 (Oberlandsgericht Stuttgart) 109
India Videogran Ltd v. Patel [1991] 1 All E.R. 214 176
Indian Grace, The [1993] A.C. 410; [1993] 1 Lloyd's Rep. 387; [1993] 1 All E.R. 998 (H.L.) 255, 267, 324, 547, 607, 608
Indian Grace, The (No. 2) [1994] 2 Lloyd's Rep. 331 ....255, 547
Indian Oil Corpn. v. Vanol Inc. [1992] 2 Lloyd's Rep. 563 (C.A.) 213, 275
Indussa Corpn. v. The Ramborg [1967] 2 Lloyd's Rep. 101 245
Industrial Diamond Supplies v. Riva (43/77) [1977] ECR 2175; [1978] 1 CMLR 349 (ECJ) 648
Industrie, The (1871) L.R. 3 A. & E. 303 52

Industrie, The [1894] P. 58 575
Industrie Tessili Italiana v. Dunlop AG (12/76) [1976] ECR 1473; [1977] 1 CMLR 26 (ECJ) 149, 150
Ines, The [1993] 2 Lloyd's Rep. 492 185
Inna, The [1938] P. 148 ....501, 502
Insurance Co. v. Lloyd's Syndicate [1995] 1 Lloyd's Rep. 272 ....283, 553
Inter Islands Exporters Ltd v. Bernia SS Ltd, 1960 S.L.T. 21 411
Interdesco SA v. Nullifire Ltd [1992] 1 Lloyd's Rep. 180 ....636, 637, 648, 650
Interpool Ltd v. Galani [1987] 2 All E.R. 981 107
Inwards v. Baker [1965] 2 Q.B. 29 458
Ion, The [1980] 2 Lloyd's Rep. 245 214
Ioannis Daskalelis (Sup. Ct. Canada) 601
Ipswich Borough Council v. Fisons plc [1990] Ch. 709; [1990] 1 All E.R. 730 (C.A.) 287
Iran Bohonar, The [1983] 2 Lloyd's Rep. 620 552
Iran Vojdan, The [1984] 2 Lloyd's Rep. 380 ....240, 575
Irish Fir, The (1943) 76 Ll.L.Rep. 51 343
Isabella, The (1838) 3 Hag. Adm. 427 66
Isabelle Lancray SA v. Peters and Sicket (C305/88) [1991] I.L.Pr. 99 (ECJ) 638
Isca, The (1886) 12 P.D. 34 ....61, 63
Ishikazi Kisen Co. Ltd v. US (18–975) AMC 287 (US Ct. of Appeals) 594
Island Archon, The [1993] 2 Lloyd's Rep. 388; [1994] 2 Lloyd's Rep. 227 (C.A.) 275
Islanders Canning Corpn. v. Hoekstra, ECD 1–17.1.1–B4 (District Ct. Leeuwarden Netherlands) 114
Israel Bank v. Hadjapateras [1983] 2 All E.R. 129 617
Italian Cargo of Adulterated Wine, Re an [1991] I.L.Pr. 473 (Oberlandsgericht Koblenz) 303
Italy II, The [1987] 2 Lloyd's Rep. 162 333
Itel Containers Corpn. v. Atlantrafik Express Service Ltd, [1992] LMLN 345 (USCA 2nd Grant) 68
Iveco Fiat SpA v. Van Hool NV (313/85) [1988] 1 CMLR 57 (ECJ) 109, 111, 112

Jacobson v. Frachon (1927) 138 L.T. 386 615
Jade, The [1976] 2 Lloyd's Rep. 1 (H.L.); [1976] 1 Lloyd's Rep. 81; [1976] 1 All E.R. 441 (C.A.); [1974]
    2 Lloyd's Rep. 188 ....21, 32, 50–52, 56–59, 61, 63, 65, 194, 195, 202
Jalamatoya, The [1987] 2 Lloyd's Rep. 164 331
James Buchanan and Co. v. Babco Forwarding and Shipping (UK) [1978] A.C. 141; [1978] 1 CMLR
    1048 88
James Miller & Partners Ltd v. Whitworth St. Estates (Manchester) Ltd [1970] A.C. 583 581
James Seddon, The (1866) 1 A. & E. 62 40
James W. Elwell, The [1921] P. 351 ....41, 336, 346, 411, 509–511
Janet Wilson, The (1857) Swab. 261 41
Jangmi, The [1989] 2 Lloyd's Rep. 1 175
Jarlinn, The [1965] 2 Lloyd's Rep. 191 335
Jarvis Brake, The [1976] 2 Lloyd's Rep. 320 ....335, 555
Jay Bola, The [1992] 2 Lloyd's Rep. 62; [1992] 3 All E.R. 329 ....174, 175, 181, 220, 225
Jeff Davis, The (1867) L.R. 2 A. & E. 1 496
Jemrix, The [1981] 2 Lloyd's Rep. 544 279
Jenmont-Schneider SA v. Ercole Marellu SpA [1994] I.L.Pr. 12 (Corte di Cassazione) 111
Jenny Lind, The (1872) L.R. 3 A. & E. 529 ....474, 503
Joannis Vatis, The (No. 2) [1992] P. 213 344
Jocelyne, The [1977] 2 Lloyd's Rep. 121 288
Jogoo, The [1981] 1 Lloyd's Rep. 513 ....337, 473
Johnny Two, The [1992] 2 Lloyd's Rep. 257 333
Johnson v. Coventry Churchill International Ltd [1992] 3 All E.R. 14 ....590, 591
Johnson v. Hill (1822) 3 Stark. 172 439
Johnson v. Shippin (1704) 1 Salk. 35 381
Johnson (S.C.) v. Mobilar Export Import GmbH [1984] ECC 360 (District Ct. Rotterdam) 628
Johnson Matthey and Wallace Ltd v. Ahmad Alloush [1985] N.L.J. 1012 (C.A.) 569
Jonathan Goodhue, The (1858) Swab. 355 399
Jones v. Trollope Colls Cementation Overseas Ltd, The Times, 26 January 1990 ....215, 570
Jordan Nicolov, The [1990] 2 Lloyd's Rep. 11 275
Jowitt v. Union Cold Storage Co. [1913] 3 K.B. 1 ....441, 444
Joyce v. Joyce [1979] 1 All E.R. 175 226
Judgment of 3 October 1978, ECD 1–5.3–B9 152
Judgment of Cour d'Appel d'Aix en Provence, 9 June (France) 527
Judgment of Court of First Instance Piraeus, No. 2505/1991 (Greece) 527

Judgment of Landgericht Aachen, 16 January 1976, ECD 1–57–B2 129
Judgment of Landgericht Aachen, 25 June 1976, ECD 1–57–B3 133
Judgment of Oberlandsgericht Karlsruhe, 1977, ECD 1–5.5–B8 238
Jugoslavenska Oceanska Plovidba v. Castle Investment Co. Inc. [1974] Q.B. 292 (C.A.) 550
Jupiter, The (No. 2) [1925] P. 69 .... 47, 266

K. H. Enterprise, The [1994] 1 Lloyd's Rep. 593 241
KS/AS Admiral Shipping v. Portlink Ferries Ltd [1984] 2 Lloyd's Rep. 166 .... 359, 498
Kahan v. Pakistan Federation [1951] 2 K.B. 1003 256
Kalamazoo, The (1851) 15 Jur. 885 382
Kaleten, The (1914) 30 T.L.R. 572 398
Kalfelis v. Schroder (189/87) [1988] ECR 5565 (ECJ) 123, 146, 151, 156
Kapetan Markos, The [1986] 1 Lloyd's Rep. 211 (C.A.) 220
Kaptein v. Van Hoasten (1978) ECD 1–21–B5 (RB The Hague) 233
Karnak, The (1869) L.R. 2 P.C. 505 40
Katcher, The (No. 2) [1968] 2 Lloyd's Rep. 29 191
Katingaki, The [1976] 2 Lloyd's Rep. 372 ....341, 440, 446
Keary v. Tarmac [1995] 3 All E.R. 533 (C.A.) 301
Kelly v. Selwyn [1905] 2 Ch. 117 571
Ketteman v. Hansel [1987] A.C. 189 .... 220, 225
Kherson, The [1992] 2 Lloyd's Rep. 261 ....242, 322, 328
Kianta Osakeyhtio v. Britain & Overseas Trading Co. Ltd [1954] 1 Lloyd's Rep. 247 291
Kleinwort Benson Ltd v. City of Glasgow DC (346/93) [1995] All E.R. (E.C.) 514 .... 85, 94
Kloebe, Re (1884) 28 Ch. D. 175 571
Klomps v. Michel (166/80) [1981] ECR 1593; [1982] 2 CMLR 773 (ECJ) 638, 639, 641
Kohn v. Rinson and Stafford (Bros.) Ltd [1947] 2 All E.R. 839 301
Komninos S, The [1990] 1 Lloyd's Rep. 541; [1991] 1 Lloyd's Rep. 370 (C.A.) 160, 215, 241,
    563, 570, 578
Kong Magnus, The [1891] P. 223 226
Kongress Agentur Hagen GmbH v. Zeehaghe BV (365/88) [1980] 1 ECR 1845 (ECJ) 157
Koop v. Bebb (1957) 84 C.L.R. 629 (High Ct. Australia) 562
Kronprinz Olav, The [1921] P. 52; (1920) 5 Ll.L.Rep. 203 535
Kurz v. Stella Musical Veranstaltungs GmbH [1992] 1 All E.R. 360 .... 108, 110
Kusu Island, The [1985] IMLJ 342 (C.A. Singapore) 209, 225
Kuwait Airways Corpn. v. Iraq Airways Co. and Republic of Iraq [1995] 2 Lloyd's Rep. 317 (H.L.);
    [1994] 1 Lloyd's Rep. 276 (C.A.) 257, 258
Kuwait Airways Corpn. v. Iraq Airways Co. (No. 2) [1995] 1 All E.R. 790 551
Kwasind, The (1915) 84 L.J.P. 102 55
Kyriaki, The [1993] 1 Lloyd's Rep. 137; [1994] 1 All E.R. 401 .... 174, 225

LTV GmbH KG v. Eurocontrol (29/76) [1976] ECR 1541; [1977] 1 CMLR 88 (ECJ) 91, 627
La Constancia (1846) 2 W. Rob. 404; 4 Not. Cas. 512 .... 44, 390
La Pintada, The [1984] 2 Lloyd's Rep. 9 (H.L.) 5, 281, 551
Ladenimn S.A. v. Intercomfinanz S.A. (314/92) (ECJ) 105
Lady Katherine Barham, The (1861) Lush 404 415
Lady Muriel, The [1995] LMLN 413 (Hong Kong) 283
Lakhta, The [1992] 2 Lloyd's Rep. 269 .... 47, 252
Lamb and Sons v. Rider [1948] 2 All E.R. 402 229
Lancaster, The [1980] 2 Lloyd's Rep. 497 ....370, 373, 440, 441, 459, 463, 468
Langen v. Bell [1972] 1 All E.R. 296 458
Laugher v. Donovon [1948] 2 All E.R. 11 229
Law Guarantee and Trust Soc. v. Russian Bank for Foreign Trade [1905] 1 K.B. 815 482
Lawson v. Midland Travellers Ltd [1993] 1 All E.R. 989 .... 189, 227
Lazenby v. McNicholas [1995] 3 All E.R. 820 291
Le Feuvre v. Sullivan (1855) 10 Moo. P.C. 1 571
Leal v. Dunlop Bio Processes Ltd [1984] 2 All E.R. 207 (C.A.) 179
Leif Hoegh and Co. A/S v. Petrolseq Inc. [1993] 1 Lloyd's Rep. 363 283
Leni, The [1992] 2 Lloyd's Rep. 48 220
Leo, The (1862) Lush. 444 398
Leoborg, The [1962] 2 Lloyd's Rep. 146 67
Leoborg, The (No. 2) [1964] 1 Lloyd's Rep. 380 ....391, 411, 473, 474, 499,
    501, 506

Leon, The (1881) 6 P.D. 148 589
Leon Blum, The [1915] P. 290 417
Leon XIII, The (1883) 8 P.D. 121 265
Leroux v. Brown (1852) 12 C.B. 801 573
Levy v. Barnard (1818) 8 Taunt. 149 443
Leyland Daf, Re [1993] B.C.C. 426 439
Liebe v. Grobel (C292/93) (ECJ) 105
Liff v. Peasley [1980] 1 All E.R. 623 225
Linda, The [1988] 1 Lloyd's Rep. 175 ....236, 238
Linda Flor, The (1857) Swab. 309 ....474, 502
Lindsay Petroleum v. Hurd (1874) L.R. 5 P.C. 221 226
Lines Bros. Ltd, Re [1983] Ch. 1 551
Lipkin Gorman v. Karpnale Ltd [1992] 4 All E.R. 512 (H.L.) 595
Lisboa, The [1980] 2 Lloyd's Rep. 546 (C.A.) 241, 268, 270, 271, 331
Lister v. Stubbs (1890) 45 Ch. D. 1 ....296, 299
Littauer Glove Corpn. v. F. W. Millington Ltd (1928) 44 T.L.R. 746 616
Livietta, The (1883) 8 P.D. 209 509
Llandovery Castle, The [1920] P. 119 214
Lloyd v. Guibert (1865) L.R. 1 Q.B. 115 597
Lloyd v. Wright [1983] 2 All E.R. 969 (C.A.) 275
Lloyd Pacifico, The [1995] 1 Lloyd's Rep. 54 ....62, 68, 71, 332
Lloydiana, The [1983] 2 Lloyd's Rep. 313 178
Lloyd's Bowmaker Ltd v. Britannia Arrow Holdings [1988] 3 All E.R. 178; [1988] 1 W.L.R. 1337 226,
                                                                                                             358, 359
Lloyd's Register of Shipping v. Société Campenon Bernard (C439/93) [1995] 1 All E.R. (E.C.) 531
    (ECJ) 154
Lombard North Central Ltd v. Lord Advocate, 1983 S.L.T. 361 490
London and Chesham v. Lapaglene [1971] Ch. 499 486
Longford, The (1889) 14 P.D. 34 (C.A.) 383
Lord Strathcona, The [1925] P. 143; [1926] A.C. 108 (H.L.) 336
Lord Warden of Cinque Ports v. R. (1831) 2 Hag. Adm. 438 49
Lorna Doon, The [1993] LMLN 367 (Australia) 527
Loucks v. Standard Oil Co., 224 N.Y. 99 (1918) 578
Lowland Yachts BV v. Firma Dahm International [1991] I.L.Pr. 350 (District Ct. The Hague) 303
Luka Botic, The [1984] 2 Lloyd's Rep. 145 (C.A.) 288
Lusitania, The [1986] Q.B. 384; [1986] 1 Lloyd's Rep. 132; [1986] 1 All E.R. 1011 ....49, 50, 399
Luz v. Bertram [1992] I.L.Pr. 537 (Corte di Cassazione) 111
Lyle Shipping v. Cardiff Corpn. [1900] 2 Q.B. 638 ....373, 462
Lyrma, The (No. 2) [1978] 2 Lloyd's Rep. 30 ....28, 298, 501–503

M Eregli, The [1981] 2 Lloyd's Rep. 169 ....280, 289
M/4 Swibon, The [1985] AMC 722 (USA) 538
MBPXL Corpn. v. International Banking Corpn. (1975) C.A. Transcript 411 352
M/S Koop, The, Re [1982] ECC 333 (Bundesgerichtshof) 150
Mac, The (1882) 7 P.D. 126 395
Macartney, Re [1921] 1 Ch. 522 615
Machinale Glasfabrieke De Maas BV v. Amaillerie Alsacienne SA [1984] ECC 124 (District Ct.
    Arnhem) 150
Maciej Rataj, The [1992] 2 Lloyd's Rep. 552 (C.A.); [1995] 1 Lloyd's Rep. 302 ..... 123, 124, 129, 156, 177,
                                                            209, 232, 235–238, 307, 430, 547, 608, 627, 631, 642
Mackender v. Feldia AG [1967] 2 Q.B. 590; [1966] 2 Lloyd's Rep. 449; [1966] 2 All E.R. 847
    (C.A.) 566, 576
Mackinnon v. Donaldson Lufkin and Jenrette Securities Ltd [1986] 1 All E.R. 653 ....78, 549
Mackinnon v. Iberia Shipping Co. Ltd, 1955 S.C. 20 (Sc.) 572, 593
Maclaine Watson v. Department of Trade [1988] 3 All E.R. 257 (C.A.) 256
Macmillan Inc. v. Bishopgate Investment Trust plc (No. 3) [1995] 3 All E.R. 747 ....568, 605
MacShannon v. Rockware Glass Ltd [1978] A.C. 795; (1978) 1 All E.R. 625 ....250, 251
Madonna D. Idra, The (1811) 1 Dods. 37 503
Maersk Nimrod, The [1992] 1 Q.B. 571; [1991] 1 Lloyd's Rep. 169 60
Maharani Woollen Mills Co. v. Anchor Line (1927) 29 Ll.L.Rep. 169 243
Maitre de Grandpu v. Ifafood SA [1993] I.L.Pr. 657 (Cour d'Appel Paris) 636
Maitre Pierrel v. Ergur [1993] I.L.Pr. 523 (Cour d'Appel, Paris) 91

Makefjell, The [1976] 2 Lloyd's Rep. 29 ....246, 247
Man (E.D. and F.) (Sugar) Ltd v. Hariyanto (No. 2) [1989] 2 Lloyd's Rep. 192 609
Manchester Ship Canal Co. v. Horlock [1914] 1 Ch. 453 454
Mangles v. Dixon (1852) 3 H.L. Cas. 702 408
Mansour v. Mansour, The Times, 2 January 1989 214
Manta Line Inc. v. Seraphim Sofianites [1984] 1 Lloyd's Rep. 14 ....177, 189
Mantovani v. Coropelli SpA [1980] 1 Lloyd's Rep. 375 268
Mara, The (formerly The Mawan) [1988] 2 Lloyd's Rep. 459 ....209, 336
Marazura Navegacion SA v. Oceanus Mutual Underwriting Association (Bermuda) Ltd [1977] 1 Lloyd's
    Rep. 283 ....271, 331
Marc Rich v. Impianti [1993] I.L.Pr. 402 (Corte di Cassazione) 94
Marc Rich and Co. AG v. Societa Italiana Impianti PA (The Atlantic Emperor) (No. 2) [1992] 1 Lloyd's
    Rep. 342; [1992] 1 Lloyd's Rep. 624 (C.A.) 92, 93, 270, 275, 276, 308, 616
Marco Reefer, The [1981] LMLN 50 555
Mardina Merchant, The [1974] 3 All E.R. 749 ....210, 333, 335, 337
Mareva Compania Navieara SA v. International Bulk Carriers SA [1975] 2 Lloyd's Rep. 509 298
Margaret Jane, The (1869) L.R. 2 A. & E. 345 338
Mari Chandris, The (1942) 71 Ll.L.Rep. 225 346
Maria Glaeser, The [1914] P. 218 393
Mariannina, The [1983] 1 Lloyd's Rep. 12 277
Marie Gartz, The (No. 2) [1920] P. 460 496
Marie Leonhardt, The [1981] 2 Lloyd's Rep. 458 ....353, 357
Marinari v. Lloyd's Bank (364/93) [1995] I.L.Pr. 737 152
Marine Contractor Inc. v. Shell Petroleum Ltd [1948] 2 Lloyd's Rep. 77 286
Marinero, The [1955] P. 68 332
Marinov, The [1995] LMLN 418 219
Maritime Harmony, The [1982] 2 Lloyd's Rep. 400 594
Maritime Trader, The [1981] 2 Lloyd's Rep. 153 ....199, 202, 284, 330
Marlex Petroleum v. The Ship Har Rai (1984) 4 D.L.R. (4th) 739 (Fed. C.A. Canada) 601
Martin Fierro, The [1974] 2 Lloyd's Rep. 203 594
Mary Ann, The (1845) 9 Jur. 94 503
Mary Ann, The (1865) L.R. 1 A. & E. 8 ....34, 428
Mason v. Uxbridge Boat Centre [1980] 2 Lloyd's Rep. 592 545
Matharu v. Matharu, The Times, 13 May 1994 458
Matija Gubec, The [1981] 1 Lloyd's Rep. 31 218
Maunns v. Henderson (1801) 1 East 335 452
Mawan, The. See Mara, The.
Mayhew Foods Ltd v. Overseas Containers Ltd [1984] 1 Lloyd's Rep. 317 563
Meadows Indemnity Co. Ltd v. Insurance Corpn. of Ireland [1989] 1 Lloyd's Rep. 181; [1989] 2 Lloyd's
    Rep. 298 (C.A.) 252, 253
Meandros, The [1925] P. 61 ....401, 405, 406
Medicale Equipex SA v. Farmitalia Erba Srl [1990] I.L.Pr. 192 (Cour d'Appel Versailles) 628, 647
Medway Packaging Ltd v. Meurer Maschinen GmbH [1990] 2 Lloyd's Rep. 112 (C.A.) 148, 151
Meeth (Nikolaus) v. Glacetal (23/78) [1978] ECR 2133; [1979] CMLR 52 (ECJ) 113
Mekhanik Egrafor, The (No. 2) [1988] 1 Lloyd's Rep. 33 528
Melanie (Owners), The v. The San Onofre (Owners) [1925] A.C. 246 28
Melbourn, Ex parte (1870) L.R. 6 Ch. App. 64 571
Menetone v. Gibbons (1789) 3 T.R. 267 ....381, 390
Merak, The [1965] 1 All E.R. 230 220
Mercantile Group (Europe) AG v. Aiyela [1994] 1 All E.R. 110 ....347, 361, 558
Mercedes Benz A.G. v. Leiduck [1995] 2 Lloyd's Rep. 417 ....299, 303, 347, 349–352, 494, 498
Mercer Co. of the City of London v. New Hampshire Insurance Co. [1992] 1 Lloyd's Rep. 431; [1992]
    2 Lloyd's Rep. 365; [1992] 3 All E.R. 57 (C.A.) 551
Mercury Communications Ltd v. DG of Telecommunications, The Times, 10 February 1995 (H.L.) 553
Mercury Publicity Ltd v. Loerke [1993] I.L.Pr. 142 (C.A.) 149, 150
Merle, The (1874) 2 Asp. M.L.C. 402 44
Messiniaki Tolmi, The [1982] Q.B. 1248 (C.A.); affirmed [1983] 2 A.C. 787; [1983] 3 W.L.R. 130
    (H.L.) 299
Messiniaki Tolmi, The [1984] 1 Lloyd's Rep. 266 (C.A.) 177, 189
Metall und Rostoff v. Donaldson Lufkin Inc. [1989] 3 All E.R. 14 588

Mikado, The [1992] 1 Lloyd's Rep. 163 ....46, 73, 298
Miliangos v. George Frank (Textiles) Ltd [1976] A.C. 443 ....550, 551
Minalmet GmbH v. Brandeis Ltd [1993] I.L.Pr. 132 (ECJ) 641
Minerva, The [1933] P. 224 32
Minna Craig Steamship Co. v. Chartered Mercantile Bank of India [1897] 1 Q.B. 55; affirmed [1897] 1
    Q.B. 460 615
Miraflores, The and the Abadesa [1976] 1 A.C. 826 52
Miramar, The [1983] 2 Lloyd's Rep. 319; [1984] 1 Lloyd's Rep. 142 (C.A.); [1984] A.C. 676; [1984] 2
    Lloyd's Rep. 129 (H.L.) 465
Miriam, The (1874) 2 Asp. M.L.C. 259 324
Missing Share Certificates, Re [1991] I.L.Pr. 298 (Oberlandsgericht Munchen) 109
Mito, The [1987] 2 Lloyd's Rep. 197 355
Mogileff, The [1921] P. 236 67
Moliere, The [1925] P. 27 55
Molnlycke AB v. Procter and Gamble Ltd [1992] 4 All E.R. 47 185
Monaco Philomel, The (1968) unreported (Fo. 414) 415
Monica S, The [1968] P. 741 ....4, 197, 430
Mons, The [1932] P. 109 ....474, 501, 503
Moorgate Mercantile Co. Ltd v. Twitchings [1976] Q.B. 225; reversed [1977] A.C. 870 ....459, 481
Moran v. Lloyd's [1983] 1 Lloyd's Rep. 51; [1983] 1 Lloyd's Rep. 472; [1983] 2 All E.R. 200
    (C.A.) 281, 286
Morley v. Hay (1829) 7 L.J.K.B. (o.s.) 104 443
Morviken, The [1983] A.C. 565; [1983] 1 Lloyd's Rep. 1 (H.L.) 81, 131, 244, 245, 254, 277, 534, 538,
                                                        565, 577, 585
Moschanthy, The [1971] 1 Lloyd's Rep. 37 ....267, 338, 342, 345, 415
Mouana, The [1991] 2 Lloyd's Rep. 441 214
Mulliner v. Florence (1878) 3 Q.B.D. 484 439
Mulox IBC Ltd v. Geels (125/92) [1993] I.L.Pr. 668 (ECJ) 149
Myerson v. Martin [1979] 3 All E.R. 667 174
Myrto, The [1977] 2 Lloyd's Rep. 243; [1978] 1 Lloyd's Rep. 11 (C.A.) 298, 337, 340, 554, 555
Myrto, The (No. 2) [1984] 2 Lloyd's Rep. 341 337
Myrto, The (No. 3) [1987] A.C. 597: [1987] 2 Lloyd's Rep. 1 (H.L) 174, 222, 227

NV Slavenburg's Bank v. Intercontinental National Resources Ltd [1980] 1 All E.R. 955 484–487
NWL Ltd v. Woods [1979] 3 All E.R. 614 297
Nagasaki Spirit, The [1994] LMLN 386 (High Ct. Singapore) 473
Nai Genova, The and The Superba [1984] 1 Lloyd's Rep. 353 552
Nanfri, The [1979] A.C. 757 ....464, 466
Napier v. Hunter [1993] 1 All E.R. 385 595
National Bank of Greece and Athens SA v. Metliss [1958] A.C. 509 215
National Iranian Oil Co. v. Banque Paribas (Suisse) [1993] LMLN 366 337
National Rumour Compania SA v. Lloyd-Libra Navegacao SA [1982] 1 Lloyd's Rep. 472 286
Naviera Amazonia Peruana v. Cie Internacional de Serguros del Peru [1988] 1 Lloyd's Rep. 116 278
Near East Relief v. King, Chasseur & Co. [1930] 2 K.B. 40 ....445, 452
Nedloyd Schie, The [1983] HKLR 17 216
Nelson, The (1805) 7 C. Rob. 227 ....44, 67
Nelson, The (1823) 1 Hag. Adm. 169 40
Nema, The [1981] 2 Lloyd's Rep. 239 ....285, 286
Neptune, The (1824) 1 Hag. Adm. 227 ....27, 390, 395
Nerano, The [1994] 2 Lloyd's Rep. 50; affirmed 15 February 1995 (C.A.) 241, 275, 279
Nestor, The (1831) 18 Fed. Cas. 9 ....381, 392
Netherlands (State of) v. Ruffer (814/79) [1980] ECR 3807; [1981] CMLR 293 (ECJ) 91, 125
New Hampshire Insurance Co. v. Strabag Bau AG [1992] 1 Lloyd's Rep. 361 (C.A.) 94, 138, 139
Newport AFC v. F.A. of Wales Ltd [1995] 2 All E.R. 87 297
Newtherapeutics Ltd v. Katz [1991] 2 All E.R. 151 184
Niceto de Larrinaga, The [1966] P. 180 221
Nichos A, The [1982] 1 Lloyd's Rep. 52 286
Niedersachsen, The [1983] 2 Lloyd's Rep. 600 (C.A.) 347, 349, 359
Niedersachsen, The (No. 2) [1986] 1 Lloyd's Rep. 393 (C.A.) 285
Nikolay Golanov, The [1994] LMLN 391 68
Nile, The (1875) 3 Asp. M.L.C. 11 263
Nile Rhapsody, The [1992] 2 Lloyd's Rep. 399; [1994] 1 Lloyd's Rep. 382 (C.A.) 245, 246, 251

Nina, The (1867) L.R. 2 A. & E. 44; on appeal (1867) L.R. 2 P.C. 38 265
Nippon Yusen Kaisha v. Karageorgis [1975] 2 Lloyd's Rep. 137 (C.A.) 298
Nishen Kisen Kaishan Ltd v. Canadian National Railway Co. [1982] 1 F.C. 530 (Fed. C.A. Canada) .. 517
Njegos, The [1936] P. 90 575
Nordglimt, The [1988] Q.B. 183; [1987] 2 Lloyd's Rep. 470; [1988] 2 All E.R. 531 .... 125, 220, 233,
                                        235, 237, 249, 307, 308, 315, 320, 383, 608
Nordstjernen, The (1857) Swab. 260 499
Norton v. Florence Land Co. (1877) 7 Ch. D. 332 571
Norwest Holst Civil Engineering Ltd v. Polysuis Ltd, The Times, 28 July 1987 356
Norwhale, The [1975] 1 Lloyd's Rep. 610 221
Norwich Pharmacal Co. v. Customs and Excise Commissioners [1974] A.C. 133 296
Nova Scotia, The [1993] 1 Lloyd's Rep. 154 ....174, 175, 181, 189
Nugent v. Smith (1875) 1 C.P.D. 19; reversed (1876) 1 C.P.D. 423 446
Nuova Raffealina, The (1871) L.R. 3 A. & E. 483 58

OHM Mariana, The Ex Peona [1993] LMLN 361 (C.A. Singapore) 198
Oakworth, The [1975] 1 Lloyd's Rep. 586 482
Ocarina Marine Ltd v. Marcaid Stein and Co. [1994] 2 Lloyd's Rep. 524 111
Ocean Blessing, The [1994] LMLN 386 (High Ct. Singapore) 334
Octavie, The (1836) B. & L. 215 ....265, 266
Oinoussin Pride, The [1991] 1 Lloyd's Rep. 126 187
Oldekerk, The [1974] 1 Lloyd's Rep. 95 594
Oldendorff v. Liberia Corpn. [1995] 2 Lloyd's Rep. 64 ....249, 566, 584
Oltenia, The [1982] 2 Lloyd's Rep. 99; [1982] 3 All E.R. 244 (C.A.) 284, 288
Omar v. Omar [1995] 3 All E.R. 571 361
Oppenheimer v. Cattermole & Co. [1976] A.C. 249; [1975] 1 All E.R. 538 (H.L.) 247, 563
Ore Chief, The [1974] 2 Lloyd's Rep. 427 594
Orienta, The [1894] P. 271 410
Orienta, The [1895] P. 39 39
Oriental, The (1851) 7 Moo. P.C. 398 407
Orpheus, The (1871) L.R. 3 A. & E. 308 398
Orri v. Moundreas [1981] Com. L.R. 168 ....200, 557
Orwell Steel v. Asphalt and Tarmac (UK) Ltd [1984] 1 W.L.R. 1097; [1985] 3 All E.R. 747 ....309, 347, 558
O'Sullivan v. Williams [1992] 3 All E.R. 385 483
Ousel, The [1957] 1 Lloyd's Rep. 151 453
Overseas Aviation Engineering (GB) Ltd, Re [1963] Ch. 24 486
Overseas Union Insurance Ltd v. New Hampshire Insurance Ltd (C351/89) [1992] 1 Lloyd's Rep. 204;
    [1992] 2 All E.R. 138 (ECJ) 96, 233
Oving Diepeveen Sturycken NV v. Berlinen Franchtschiffart [1983] ELD 361 156
Owen v. Pugh [1995] 3 All E.R. 345 228
Owenbaren, The [1973] 1 Lloyd's Rep. 56 222
Owens Bank v. Bracco [1992] 2 A.C. 443; [1992] 2 All E.R. 193 (H.L.) 107, 615, 618, 629
Owens Bank Ltd v. Bracco (No. 2) (C129/92) [1994] Q.B. 509; [1994] 1 All E.R. 336 (ECJ) 95

PCW (Underwriting Agencies) Ltd v. Dixon [1983] 2 All E.R. 158; [1983] 2 All E.R. 697 (C.A.) 298,
                                                                                                                   348
Pacific, The (1864) B. & L. 243 390
Pacific Bear, The [1979] HKLR 125 ....208, 323
Paczy (Janos) v. Haendler & Natermann GmbH [1981] 1 Lloyd's Rep. 302 280
Panama, The (1870) L.R. 3 P.C. 199 407
Panda, The (1842) 1 W. Rob. 423 49
Panglobal Friendship, The [1978] 1 Lloyd's Rep. 368 ....372, 373, 468
Paola D'Alesio, The [1994] 2 Lloyd's Rep. 366 189
Papadopoulos v. Papadopoulos [1930] P. 55 614
Paragon Ltd v. Burnell [1991] 2 All E.R. 388 174
Paramount Airways Ltd, Re [1992] 3 All E.R. 1 564
Pardo v. Bingham (1868) L.R. 6 Eq. 485 571
Paris, The [1896] P. 77 496
Parlement Belge, The (1880) 5 P.D. 197 ....404, 405
Parouth, The [1982] 2 Lloyd's Rep. 351 ....277, 566, 576, 579
Partenreederei MS Tilly Russ v. Haven and Vervoerbedrijf "Nova" and Germaine Hout (71/83) [1984]
    ECR 2417; [1984] 3 CMLR 499 (ECJ) 111, 112, 114, 115, 157

Paschalis v. The Ship Tona Maria [1975] 1 Cyp. L.R. 162 40
Pascoe v. Turner [1979] 1 W.L.R. 131 458
Pavlings Settlement Trusts, Re [1963] 3 All E.R. 1 226
Pearce, Re [1919] 1 K.B. 354 557
Pegasus, The [1967] 1 Lloyd's Rep. 303 288
Pemberton v. Hughes [1899] 1 Ch. 781 614
Pendrecht, The [1980] 2 Lloyd's Rep. 56 288
Pendy Plastic Products v. Pluspunkt Handelsgesellschaft Mbh (228/81) [1983] 1 CMLR 665 (ECJ) 637
Penelope II, The [1980] 2 Lloyd's Rep. 17 528
Perfetto v. Parlapiano [1993] I.L.Pr. 190 (Cour d'Appel Liege) 111
Permina 108, The [1978] 1 Lloyd's Rep. 311 (C.A. Singapore) 202, 314
Permina 3001, The [1979] 1 Lloyd's Rep. 327 (C.A. Singapore) 155, 199, 200, 552
Permina Samudra XIV, The [1978] 1 Lloyd's Rep. 315 ....322, 479
Petereit v. Babcock International Holdings Ltd [1990] 2 All E.R. 135 ....647, 650
Peters v. ZNAV (34/82) [1983] ECR 987; [1984] 2 CMLR 605 (ECJ) 145–147
Petone, The [1917] P. 198 ....40, 408, 409, 411
Petr Scmidt, The [1995] 1 Lloyd's Rep. 202 275
Petromin SA v. Secnav Marine Ltd [1995] 1 Lloyd's Rep. 603 ....282, 331
Philippine Admiral, The [1977] A.C. 373 257
Photo Production Ltd v. Securicor Transport Ltd [1980] A.C. 827 553
Phrantzes v. Argenti [1960] 2 Q.B. 19 ....549, 572
Pia Vesta, The [1984] 1 Lloyd's Rep. 169 177
Pickaninny, The [1960] 1 Lloyd's Rep. 544 474
Pionier, The [1995] 1 Lloyd's Rep. 223 220
Pitsa T, The [1987] 2 Lloyd's Rep. 404 ....357, 358, 363
Po, The [1991] 2 Lloyd's Rep. 206 (C.A.) 103, 125, 128, 156, 206, 233, 307, 316, 319
Polly Peck International v. Citibank NA [1994] I.L.Pr. 71 ....170, 238
Polly Peck International plc v. Asil Nadir [1992] 2 Lloyd's Rep. 238 (C.A.) 358
Polo II, The [1977] 2 Lloyd's Rep. 115 ....23, 345, 415
Polpen Shipping Co. v. Commercial Union Assurance Co. Ltd [1943] K.B. 161 395
Polypetrol v. Société Générale Routière [1993] I.L.Pr. 107 (Cour de Cassation France) 636, 641
Poomac Sprl v. SA Sogoservice [1993] I.L.Pr. 309 236
Port Caledonia, The and The Anna [1903] P. 184 596
Port Line v. Ben Line Steamers Ltd [1958] 2 Q.B. 146; [1958] 1 Lloyd's Rep. 290 ......455, 482, 603
Port Victoria, The [1902] P. 25 32
Porta Leasing GmbH v. Prestige International SA (784/79) [1980] ECR 1517; [1981] 1 CMLR 135
    (ECJ) 111, 117
Porzelack v. Porzelack [1987] 1 All E.R. 1074 ....301, 308
Potoi Chau, The [1983] 2 Lloyd's Rep. 376 218
Potts, Re [1893] 1 Q.B. 648 557
Powell Duffryn plc v. Petereit (C214/89) [1992] ECR 1745; The Times, 15 April 1992 (ECJ) 91, 109, 111
Powstaniec Wielkopolski, The [1989] 1 Lloyd's Rep. 58 31
Practice Direction [1976] 1 W.L.R. 83 551
Practice Direction [1979] 2 All E.R. 155 177
Practice Direction [1982] 2 W.L.R. 660 555
Practice Direction (Arbitration Award: Appeal) [1985] 2 All E.R. 383 ....285, 287
Practice Direction [1989] 3 All E.R. 562 186
Practice Direction [1994] 4 All E.R. 52 ....355–357, 363, 364
Prekookeanska Plovidba v. LNT Lines Spl [1988] 3 All E.R. 897 353
Preveze, The [1973] 1 Lloyd's Rep. 202 221
Prince Abdul Rahman v. Abu-Taha [1980] 2 Lloyd's Rep. 565 352
Prince George, The (1837) 3 Hag. Adm. 376 ....35, 38
Princess Alice, The (1849) 3 W. Rob. 138 66
Prinsengracht, The [1993] 1 Lloyd's Rep. 41 ....108, 178, 209, 307, 342, 343
Priscilla, The (1859) Lush. 1 504
Promac Sprl v. SA Sogeservice [1993] I.L.Pr. 309 (Cour d'Appel Paris) 148
Puerto Acevedo, The [1978] 1 Lloyd's Rep. 38 220
Pugsley & Co. v. Ropkins & Co. [1892] 2 Q.B. 184 61
Putbus, The [1969] P. 136 339

Queen of the South, The [1968] P. 449; [1968] 1 Lloyd's Rep. 182 ....22, 51, 61, 63, 67, 68, 195, 335,
                                                                                            346, 453, 454, 473, 509

R. v. Forty Nine Casks of Brandy (1836) Hag. Adm. 257 49
R. v. Judge of the City of London Court (1883) 12 Q.B.D. 115 57
R. v. Judge of City of London Court [1892] 1 Q.B. 273 390
R. v. Judge of City of London Court and Owners of S.S. Michigan (1890) 25 Q.B.D. 339 38
R. v. Property Derelict (1825) 1 Hag. Adm. 383 49
Radiant, The [1958] 2 Lloyd's Rep. 596 520
Raeburn v. Andrews (1874) L.R. 9 Q.B. 118 301
Rainbow, The (1885) 5 Asp. M.L.C. 479 417
Ralli Bros. v. Compania Naviera Sota y Aznar [1920] 2 K.B. 287 577
Rank Film Distributors v. Lanterna Editrice Srl [1992] I.L.Pr. 57 ....148, 149, 233
Rasu Maritima SA v. Perusahaan Pertambangan Minyak Dan Gas Bumi Negara (Pertamina) and
    Government of Indonesia (Intervener) [1978] Q.B. 644 ....298, 347, 353, 358
Ratna Vandana, The [1982] 1 Lloyd's Rep. 499 289
Rebecca, The (1804) 5 C. Rob. 102 408
Red Sea Insurance Co. Ltd v. Bouygues SA [1994] 3 All E.R. 749 (P.C.) 590, 591
Reefer Creole, The [1994] 1 Lloyd's Rep. 584 187
Reich v. Purcell, 432 P. 2d 727 (1967) 590
Reichert v. Dresdner Bank (115/88) [1990] I.L.Pr. 105 (ECJ) 104
Reichert v. Dresdner Bank (No. 2) (261/90) [1992] I.L.Pr. 404, 26 March 1992 (ECJ) 107, 151
Rena K, The [1979] Q.B. 377; [1978] 1 Lloyd's Rep. 545; [1979] 1 All E.R. 397 ....210, 249, 250, 280,
                    284, 299, 308, 327–329, 338, 351, 353, 413, 548
Rene, The (1922) 12 Ll.L.Rep. 202 506
Republica de Guatemala v. Nunez [1927] 1 K.B. 669 571
Rewia, The [1991] 2 Lloyd's Rep. 325 (C.A.) 120, 241
Rhodian River, The [1984] 1 Lloyd's Rep. 373 552
Ring, The [1931] P. 58 342
Ringdove, The (1858) Swab. 310 398
Rinkau (159/80) [1981] ECR 1; [1983] 1 CMLR 205 (ECJ) 155
Ripon City, The [1897] P. 226 ....39, 40, 41, 403–407, 410
River Rima, The [1988] 2 Lloyd's Rep. 193 (H.L.) 5, 10, 62, 68
Robert Pow, The (1863) B. & L. 99 52
Roberta, The [1928] P. 1 342
Roberta, The (1937) 58 Ll.L.Rep. 159 573
Roebuck v. Mungovin [1994] 1 All E.R. 568 (H.L.) 228
Roecliff, The (1869) L.R. 2 A. & E. 363 398
Rohr S.A. v. Ossberger (27/81) [1981] ECR 2431; [1982] 3 CMLR 29 (ECJ) 108
Rohstoff Einfuhr v. La Continentale Nucléaire (1977) ECD 1–22–B1 (Cour Suspencion de Justice
    Lux) 238
Romalpa Case [1976] 1 All E.R. 552 ....475, 552
Rome v. Punjab National Bank, The Times, 14 July 1988 78
Rome v. Punjab National Bank (No. 2) [1990] 1 All E.R. 58 (C.A.) 176
Rosario, The (1866) 2 P.D. 41 410
Rosco BV v. Fraisgel [1986] ECC 175 641
Rose, Re [1952] Ch. 499 476
Rosler v. Rottwinkel [1985] ECR 9 (ECJ) 105
Rosseel NV v. Oriental Commercial and Shipping Co. (UK) Ltd [1991] 2 Lloyd's Rep. 625; [1991] 1 All
    E.R. 545 ....275, 354, 622
Rosso, The [1982] 2 Lloyd's Rep. 120 ....564, 578
Royal Arch, The (1857) Swab. 269 ....40, 41, 417
Royal Bank of Scotland v. Cassa di Risparmia [1991] I.L.Pr. 411 150
Royal Wells, The [1984] 2 Lloyd's Rep. 255 ....38, 503
Ruapehu, The (1927) 27 Ll.L.Rep. 385 (H.L.) 545
Rubi Sea, The [1992] 1 Lloyd's Rep. 634 ....335, 473
Russland, The [1924] P. 55 ....342, 498, 502

SA CNV v. S GmbH [1991] I.L.Pr. 588 (Oberlandsgericht Koblenz) 233
SA Consortium General Textiles v. Sun and Sand Agencies Ltd [1978] Q.B. 279 618
SA Continental Pharma v. SA Labaz (1978) ECD 1–38–B3 (Brussels) 648
SCAC (Transport) (USA) Inc. v. Adriatica SpA di Navigazione, 1982 ECD 457 150
SCF Finance Co. Ltd v. Masri [1985] 2 All E.R. 747 347
SCF Finance Co. Ltd v. Masri (No. 3) [1987] 1 All E.R. 194 ....547, 557

SCOR v. Eras Eil (No. 2). See Société Commerciale de Reassurance v. ERAS International Ltd (No. 2).
SL Sethia Liners Ltd v. State Trading Corpn. [1986] 1 Lloyd's Rep. 31; [1986] 2 All E.R. 395   280
SNI Aerospatiale v. Lee Kui Jak [1987] 3 All E.R. 510 (P.C.)   269
Sabine, The [1974] 1 Lloyd's Rep. 465   594
Sadler v. Robins (1808) 1 Camp. 253   615
Saetta, The [1993] 2 Lloyd's Rep. 268; [1994] 1 All E.R. 851 ....46, 397, 461, 554
Saint Anna, The [1983] 1 Lloyd's Rep. 637 ....59, 64, 210, 291, 324, 548
St Elefterio, The [1957] P. 179 ....56, 58, 196, 437
St George, The [1926] P. 217 ....   40, 41
St Lawrence, The (1880) L.R. 5 P.D. 250 ....   44, 411
St Merriel, The [1963] P. 247; [1963] 1 All E.R. 537 ....43, 45, 47, 196, 204, 428, 437
St Olaf, The (1869) L.R. 2 A. & E. 360   396
St Olaf, The (1877) 2 P.D. 113   46
Saipen SpA v. Dredging VO2 BV and Geosite Surveys Ltd. See Volvox Hollandia, The.
Sakana v. Freyre [1994] 1 Lloyd's Rep. 57   549
Salacia, The (1862) Lush. 545 ....398, 503
Salvesen v. Admin. of Austrian Property [1927] A.C. 641   613
Samarkand, The [1995] LMLN 419   61
Sandalion, The [1983] 1 Lloyd's Rep. 514   288
Sanders v. Van der Putte (73/77) [1978] 1 CMLR 331 (ECJ)   105
Sanders Lead Co. Inc. v. Entores Metal Brokers Ltd [1984] 1 Lloyd's Rep. 276 ....347, 363
Sandrina, The [1985] A.C. 255; [1985] 1 Lloyd's Rep. 181 ....59, 60, 62, 66
Sanicentral v. Collin (25/79) [1979] ECR 3423; [1980] 2 CMLR 164 (ECJ) 91, 110
Santa Maria, The (1917) 36 D.L.R. 619   44
Sante Fe (UK) Ltd v. Gates Europe [1991] LMLN 295 ....151, 162
Saqr Jubail, The [1985] LMLN 140   338
Sara, The (1889) 14 App.Cas. 209 ....26, 33, 34, 428
Sarah Bell, The (1864) 4 Not. Cas. 144   399
Sargasso, The [1994] 2 Lloyd's Rep. 6 (C.A.) 108, 233, 235, 305, 315, 320, 343, 349
Sarpen, The [1916] P. 306   263
Saudi Prince, The [1982] 2 Lloyd's Rep. 255   200
Saudi Star, The (1982) unreported 342–344
Savina, The [1975] 2 Lloyd's Rep. 141   594
Sayers v. International Drilling Co. NV [1971] 2 Lloyd's Rep. 105; [1971] 3 All E.R. 163 .... 564, 574,
                                                                                        577, 589, 593
Scan Expo Wortmann GmbH v. Ringkøbing County [1994] I.L.Pr. 335 (Western C.A. Denmark) 111, 146
Scaptrade, The [1983] 2 All E.R. 763   552
Schimmel Pianoforkfabrik GmbH v. Hubert Bion [1992] I.L.Pr. 199 (Cour de Cassation)   152
Scio, The (1867) L.R. 1 A. & E. 353 ....440, 497
Sea Spray, The [1907] P. 133   473
Sea Cap XII, The [1995] LMLN 415 (F.C.)   517
Seaconsar Far East Ltd v. Bank Markasi Iran [1993] 4 All E.R. 456 (H.L.) 181, 188
Searose Ltd v. Seatrain (UK) Ltd [1981] 1 Lloyd's Rep. 556   357
Seaspeed America, The [1990] 1 Lloyd's Rep. 150   222
Seaspeed Dora, The [1988] 1 Lloyd's Rep. 36; [1987] 3 All E.R. 967 (C.A.)   301
Secretary of State for the Environment v. Euston Castle Investments Ltd [1994] 2 All E.R. 415   287
Securities and Investments Board v. Lloyd-Wright [1993] 4 All E.R. 210   355
Sedex v. Société Vetex [1990] I.L.Pr. 254 (Cour de Cassation)   148
Selina, The (1842) 2 Not. Cas. 18   504
Sennar, The (No. 2) [1985] 1 Lloyd's Rep. 521 (H.L.) 241, 255
Servia and Carinthia, The [1898] P. 36   44
Sewell v. Burdick (1884) 10 App.Cas. 74 ....492, 495
Shearson Lehman Hutton Inc. v. TVB (89/91) [1993] I.L.Pr. 199 (ECJ) 123, 143
Sheba, The and The Shamson [1983] 2 Lloyd's Rep. 500   286
Sheldon v. Outhwaite [1995] 2 All E.R. 558 (H.L.)   223
Shell Oil Co. v. The Ship Lastrigoni (1974–75) 131 C.L.R. 1 (High Ct. Australia)   434
Shenavai v. Kreischer (266/85) [1987] 3 CMLR 782 (ECJ) 148, 149
Shevill v. Presse Alliance SA (68/93) [1995] All E.R. (E.C.) 289 (ECJ)   152
Ship Galaxias, The [1989] LMLN 240 (Fed. Ct. Canada)   555
Shizelle, The [1992] 2 Lloyd's Rep. 445 ....480, 489, 490, 500, 504, 507
Shopfitting Contract, Re a [1993] I.L.Pr. 393 (Oberlandsgericht Saarbrucken)   108

Showlag v. Mansour [1994] 2 All E.R. 129 (P.C.) 609
Siamar v. Spedimex [1990] I.L.Pr. 266 (Sup. Ct. Italy) 127
Siben, The [1994] 2 Lloyd's Rep. 420 (C.A. Jersey) 46
Sierra Nevada, The (1932) 42 Ll.L.Rep. 309 508
Silia, The [1981] 2 Lloyd's Rep. 534; [1981] LMLN 36 ....37, 69, 394–396, 435, 510, 554
Sim Swee Joo v. Shirlstar [1994] LMLN 374 273
Simlah, The (1851) 18 L.T. (O.S.) 35 417
Simon v. Taylor [1975] 2 Lloyd's Rep. 338 27
Simonds v. White (1824) 2 B. & C. 805 597
Sing v. Duport Foundries Ltd [1994] 2 All E.R. 889 (C.A.) 175
Sinoe, The [1972] 1 Lloyd's Rep. 201 (C.A.) 469
Sion v. Hampstead Health Authority, *The Times*, 10 June 1994 ....224, 225
Siporex Trade SA v. Comdel Commodities Ltd [1986] 2 Lloyd's Rep. 428 ....350, 358
Siskina, The [1979] A.C. 210; [1978] 1 Lloyd's Rep. 1 (H.L.) 184, 185, 350, 351
Skaw Prince, The [1994] LMLN 390 (High Ct. Singapore) 200
Skinner v. Upshaw (1702) 2 Ld. Ray. 752 447
Skylark, The [1965] 2 Lloyd's Rep. 250 48
Slavenburg Case. *See* NV Slavenburg's Bank v. Intercontinental National Resources Ltd.
Smith v. Peters (1875) 299
Soc. Sectom v. Soc. Fremo (1981) 1982 ECD 230 (Cass. Civ. Italy) 636
Societa Kretschmer v. Muratoir (Corte di Cassazione) [1991] I.L.Pr. 361 148
Société Biomécanique Integue Fabrique National de Heutal SA [1993] I.L.Pr. 227 641
Société Commerciale de Reassurance v. ERAS International Ltd [1992] 1 Lloyd's Rep. 570; [1992] 3 All
    E.R. 82 (C.A.) 215
Société Commerciale de Reassurance v. ERAS International Ltd (No. 2) [1995] 2 All E.R. 278 268,
    269, 297
Société d'Informatique Service Realisation Organisation v. Ampersand Software BV (432/93) [1995] All
    E.R. (E.C.) 783 ....636, 647
Société Gola Werke Gotz KG v. André Barseghian (1979) ECD 1–5.1.2–B25 (Cour d'Appel Lyon) 109
Société Launay v. Deyglat (1979) ECD 1–28–B2 (Cour d'Appel Orleans) 634
Société Leybold v. Seima, 1978 ECD 1–6–B3 156
Société Montedison v. Departement de la Haute Corse (1977) ECD 1–5.3–B3 (Court d'Appel
    Bastia) 238
Soeraya Emas, The [1992] LMLN 338 (High Ct. Singapore) 209
Sohio Supply Co. v. Gatoil [1989] 1 Lloyd's Rep. 585 242
Sokana Industries Inc. v. Frere and Co. Inc. [1994] 2 Lloyd's Rep. 57 283
Soleh Bonah International v. Government of Uganda and National Housing Corpn. [1993] 2 Lloyd's Rep.
    208 (C.A.) 257
Solo Kleinmotoren GmbH v. Boch (414/92) [1994] I.L.Pr. 457 (ECJ) 627
Somafer SA v. Saar Ferngas AG (33/78) [1978] ECR 2183; [1979] 1 CMLR 490 (ECJ) 123, 145,
    146, 153, 154
Somes v. British Empire Shipping Co. (1860) 8 H.L. Cas. 338 440
Sonia S., The [1983] 1 Lloyd's Rep. 63 61
Sonntag v. Waidmann (172/91) 21 April 1993 (ECJ) 627
South Carolina Insurance Co. v. Assurantie Maatschappij [1986] 2 Lloyd's Rep. 317 (H.L.) 268
Span Terza, The [1982] 1 Lloyd's Rep. 225 (C.A.) 51, 195, 198, 202, 203, 314, 328
Span Terza, The (No. 2) [1982] 2 Lloyd's Rep. 72; reversed on a construction point [1984] 1 Lloyd's
    Rep. 199 (H.L) 555
Spears v. Hartley (1800) 3 Esp. 81 444
Spedag Scheepvaart en Expeditiebedrijf BV v. Andria Reederei GmbH and Co. KG [1986] ELD 206
    (R. B. Rotterdam) 111
Spermina, The (1923) 17 Ll.L.Rep. 52 509
Spiliada, The [1987] A.C. 460; [1987] 1 Lloyd's Rep. 1; [1986] 3 All E.R. 843 (H.L.) 181, 182, 185,
    186, 188, 189, 216, 248, 251–253, 532, 534–536
Staat Der Nederlanden v. Partenreederei Erata [1986] ELD 207 (Hof The Hague) 235
Staffordshire, The (1872) L.R. 4 P.C. 194; 1 Asp. M.L.C. 365 ....342, 398
Stainbank v. Fenning (1851) 11 C.B. 51 ....41, 407
Stainbank v. Shepard (1853) 13 C.B. 418 ....41, 407, 416
Stapleton v. Hayman (1864) 2 H. & C. 918 479
Star of Luxor, The [1981] 1 Lloyd's Rep. 139 246
Star Texas, The [1993] 2 Lloyd's Rep. 445 (C.A.) 240, 277, 575, 579–581, 597
Steamship Mutual Underwriting Association (Bermuda) Ltd [1986] 2 Lloyd's Rep. 439 350

Steedman v. Schofield [1992] 2 Lloyd's Rep. 163 ....27, 221, 395
Stella Nova, The [1981] Comm. L.R. 200 ....59, 61, 64, 324, 351, 548
Stena Nautica, The (No. 2) [1982] 2 Lloyd's Rep. 336 ....479, 552
Stena Pacifica, The [1990] 2 Lloyd's Rep. 234 275
Stephan J, The [1985] 2 Lloyd's Rep. 344 ....207, 322
Stockport Metropolitan Borough Council v. O'Reilly [1983] 2 Lloyd's Rep. 70 ....281, 288
Stolt Filia, The [1980] LMLN 15 ....351, 556
Stolt Loyalty, The [1995] 1 Lloyd's Rep. 598 (C.A.) 214
Straithaird Farms Ltd v. Chattaway, 1993 SLT (Sh. Ct.) 36 ....147, 162
Strang Steel & Co. v. Scott (1889) 14 App.Cas. 601 451
Strathnaver, The (1875) 1 App.Cas. 58 337
Strathnewton, The [1983] 1 Lloyd's Rep. 219 214
Stream Fisher, The [1927] P. 73; 26 Ll.L.Rep. 4 ....32, 502, 506
Struma, The [1978] AMC 2146 603
Subleuse of a Shop, Re [1991] I.L.Pr. 292 (Oberlandsgericht Dusseldorf) 108
Sullivar, The [1965] 2 Lloyd's Rep. 350 554
Swan v. Barber (1879) 5 Ex. D. 130 447
Syal v. Heyward [1948] 2 K.B. 443 615
Sydney Cove, The (1815) 2 Dods. 11 ....35, 503
Sydney Express, The [1988] 2 Lloyd's Rep. 257 108
Sylph, The (1867) L.R. 2 A. & E. 24 33
Sylt, The [1991] 1 Lloyd's Rep. 240 ....330, 331, 614
Sylt, The [1993] LMCLQ 433 (Sup. Ct. Holland) 538
Sylvan Arrow, The [1923] P. 14 ....405, 406
Synova, The [1976] 1 Lloyd's Rep. 40 335
Systemica Ltd v. London Computer Centre Ltd [1983] FSR 313 297
Szalatray-Stacho v. Fink [1947] 1 K.B. 1 588

TDK Distributors (UK) Ltd v. Videochoice Ltd [1985] 3 All E.R. 345 352
TSM Compagnie D'Assurances Transports v. Geisseler Transport AG [1993] I.L.Pr. 61 (Hoge Raad
    Netherlands) 132
Tacoma City, The [1991] 1 Lloyd's Rep. 330 (C.A.) 37
Taggert Beaton & Co. v. James Fisher and Sons [1903] 1 K.B. 391 466
Tagus, The [1903] P. 44 ....40, 411, 571
Talamba, The [1965] 2 All E.R. 775 415
Tappenden v. Artus [1964] 2 Q.B. 185 ....442, 447
Tasmania, The (1888) 13 P.D. 110 404
Tatiangela, The [1980] 2 Lloyd's Rep. 193 358
Tehno-Impex v. Gebr. van Weelde Scheepvaartkantoor B.V. [1981] 1 Q.B. 648; [1981] 1 Lloyd's Rep.
    587 (C.A.) 5, 278
Tenacia, The [1982] LMLN 55 575
Tergeste, The [1903] P. 26 ....440, 443, 497, 498
Tervaete, The [1922] P. 259 ....401, 404–406, 412
Tesaba, The [1982] 1 Lloyd's Rep. 397 ....56, 61–63, 65, 66
Tesam Distribution Ltd v. Schuh-Mode Team GmbH [1990] I.L.Pr. 149 (C.A.) 148
Texaco Ltd v. Eurogulf Shipping Co. [1987] LMLN 194 280
Texaco Southampton, The [1983] 1 Lloyd's Rep. 94 (C.A. NSW) 27
Tharros Shipping Co. v. Bias Shipping Ltd [1994] 1 Lloyd's Rep. 577 356
Themehelp v. West [1995] 4 All E.R. 215 (C.A.) 297
Theotokos, The [1983] 2 Lloyd's Rep. 204 ....360, 362–364
Theta, The [1894] P. 280 32
Thierry Noirhomme v. David Walklate [1992] 1 Lloyd's Rep. 427 ....187, 638, 639, 648
Third Chandris Shipping Corpn. v. Unimarine SA [1979] Q.B. 645 ....347, 352, 359
Thompson v. Brown Construction (Ebbw Vale) Ltd [1981] 2 All E.R. 296 (H.L.) 223, 228
Thompson v. H. and W. Nelson [1913] 2 K.B. 523 38
Three Rivers D.C. v. Bank of England [1995] All E.R. 312 493
Thune v. London Properties Ltd [1990] 1 All E.R. 972 (C.A.) 301, 302
Ticonderoga, The (1857) Swab. 215 403
Tobago, The (1804) 5 C. Rob. 218 ....41, 393
Tojo Maru, The [1972] A.C. 242 28
Tolley v. Morris [1979] 1 W.L.R. 592 228
Tolten, The [1946] P. 135 ....32, 34, 264, 589, 599

Toluca, The [1981] 2 Lloyd's Rep. 548 594
Toprak v. Sale Tilney Technology plc [1994] 3 All E.R. 483 225
Tor Britannia, The [1982] 1 Lloyd's Rep. 410 277
Tracomin SA v. Sudan Oil Seeds (No. 1) [1983] 3 All E.R. 137 616
Trade Indemnity v. Forsakrings AB [1995] 1 All E.R. 796 148
Trans Atlantica SpA v. Vertom Shipping 1984 ELD 393 (Italy) 640
Transoceanica Francesca, The [1987] 2 Lloyd's Rep. 15 551
Traugutt, The [1985] 1 Lloyd's Rep. 76 566
Trendtex Trading Corpn. v. Central Bank of Nigeria [1977] Q.B. 529; [1977] 1 All E.R. 881 .... 256, 262
Trendtex Trading Corpn. v. Crédit Suisse [1980] Q.B. 629; [1980] 3 All E.R. 721 (C.A.) affirmed [1982]
    A.C. 679; [1981] 3 All E.R. 520 (H.L.) 241, 245–248, 408, 493
Trepca Mines, Re [1960] 1 W.L.R. 1273 617
Trident Beauty, The [1994] 1 Lloyd's Rep. 365 (H.L.) 595
Trill v. Sacher [1993] 1 All E.R. 961 (C.A.) 228
Troll River, The [1974] 2 Lloyd's Rep. 181 594
Tropwave, The [1981] 2 Lloyd's Rep. 159 469
Troubadour, The (1866) L.R. 1 A. & E. 302 390
Tsai v. Woodworth (1983) 127 S.J. 858; The Times, 30 November 1983 (C.A.) 173, 222
Tubantia, The [1924] P. 78 22
Turkiye Is Bankasi SA v. Bank of China [1993] 1 Lloyd's Rep. 132 575
Tuyuti, The [1984] 2 Lloyd's Rep. 51; [1984] 2 All E.R. 545 .... 249, 250, 284, 300, 302,
                                                                          308, 327, 329, 330, 338
Two Ellens, The (1871) L.R. 3 A. & E. 345 (C.A.); (1872) L.R. 4 P.C. 161 (P.C.) 33, 390, 479, 499
Two Friends, The (1799) 1 C. Rob. 271 .... 381, 390
Tyburn Productions v. Conan Doyle [1991] Ch. 75 78

US Steel Products Co. v. G.W. Rly. Co. [1916] 1 A.C. 189 445
Ugha Group v. NVBSL (1979) ECD 1–22–B2 (Hof van Beroep Belgium) 233
Ugland Obo One, the [1986] 2 Lloyd's Rep. 336; [1986] 3 All E.R. 737 287
Ugland Trailer, The [1985] 2 Lloyd's Rep. 372 ....370, 458, 466, 485, 487
Union, The (1860) Lush. 128 503
Union Bank of London v. Lenanton (1878) 3 C.P.D. 243 .... 479, 600
Union Insurance v. SS Elikon [1982] AMC 588 245
Union International Insurance Co. Ltd v. Jubilee Insurance Co. Ltd [1991] 2 Lloyd's Rep. 89 184
Union Nationale des Cooperatives Agricoles v. Catterall [1959] 2 Q.B. 44 621
Union of India v. McDonnell Douglas Corpn. [1993] 2 Lloyd's Rep. 48 ....278, 581
Union Transport Group Plc v. Continental Lines SA [1992] 1 All E.R. 161 (H.L.) 148
Unique Mariner, The (No. 2) [1979] 1 Lloyd's Rep. 37 28
Unisys International Services Ltd v. Eastern Counties Newspapers Ltd [1991] 1 Lloyd's Rep. 508 290
United Railways of Havana and Regla Warehouses Ltd, Re [1960] Ch. 52 (C.A.) 576
Universe Tankships v. ITF [1982] 2 All E.R. 67 (H.L.) 266
Utopia, The [1893] A.C. 492 (P.C.) 51, 404, 405

Vadala v. Lawes (1890) 25 Q.B.D. 310 615
Van Dalfsen v. Van Loon (183/90) [1992] I.L.Pr. 5 (ECJ) 626, 648, 652
Van Eijk and Zoon-Somerville [1906] A.C. 489 516
Van Rolleghem v. Roth, 22 March 1979, ECD 1–1.2–B5 (Trib. de Commerce, Brussels) 91
Vanessa Ann, The [1985] 1 Lloyd's Rep. 549 ....46, 339, 340, 432
Varna, The [1993] 2 Lloyd's Rep. 253 ....196, 300, 322, 327, 328, 332
Varna, The (No. 2) [1994] 2 Lloyd's Rep. 41 ....253, 430
Vasilia, The [1972] 1 Lloyd's Rep. 51 ....411, 554
Vasso, The [1983] 2 Lloyd's Rep. 346 ....281, 283
Vasso, The (formerly The Andria) [1984] 1 Lloyd's Rep. 235; [1984] A.C. 293; [1984] 1 All E.R. 1126
    (C.A.) 197, 249, 268, 322, 327
Vaz Borralho v. Keydril, 696 F.2d 379 (1983) (US Court of Appeals, 5th Circuit) 248
Vera Cruz, The (No. 2) (1884) 10 App.Cas. 59 (H.L.) 34
Vera Cruz I, The [1992] 1 Lloyd's Rep. 353 350
Veritas, The [1901] P. 304 ....26, 28, 32, 33, 501, 502
Vestland, The [1980] 2 Lloyd's Rep. 171 ....336, 468
Victor, The (1860) Lush. 72 398
Victrix Steamship Co. SA v. Salen Dry Cargo AB, 1987 AMC 276 (SDNY) 92

Vikfrost, The [1980] 1 Lloyd's Rep. 560 279
Virgin Aviation Services Ltd v. CAD Aviation Services [1991] I.L.Pr. 79; [1991] I.L.Pr. 448 ....233, 238, 628
Virgo, The [1978] 2 Lloyd's Rep. 16; [1978] 3 All E.R. 988 288
Vishva Abha, The [1990] 2 Lloyd's Rep. 312 ....253, 254, 517, 534
Vishva Ajay, The [1989] 2 Lloyd's Rep. 558 253
Vita, The [1990] 1 Lloyd's Rep. 528 .... 174, 214
Vita Food Products Inc. v. Unus Shipping Co. Ltd [1939] A.C. 277 ....575, 577, 585
Vitol SA v. Norelf Ltd [1995] 1 All E.R. 971 (C.A.) 285
Volker Sonntag v. Hans Waidmann (C172/91) 21 April 1993 (ECJ) 640, 652
Volvox Hollandia, The [1989] ECC 16 532–535
Vrontados, The [1982] 2 Lloyd's Rep. 241 ....174, 180, 187, 214

WEA Records Ltd v. Visions Channel 4 Ltd [1983] 2 All E.R. 589 300
Waddon v. Whitecroft Scovell Ltd [1988] 1 All E.R. 996 (H.L.) 174, 175, 227
Wagner v. Tettweiler [1985] ECC 258 (Cour de Cassation France) 637
Wahda Bank v. Arab Bank plc [1994] 2 Lloyd's Rep. 411 575
Wait, Re [1927] 1 Ch. 606 ....200, 458, 476
Walkley v. Precision Forgings Ltd [1979] 2 All E.R. 548 223
Wardens of The Mercers of London v. New Hampshire Insurance Co. [1992] 1 Lloyd's Rep. 431; [1992]
    2 Lloyd's Rep. 365; [1992] 3 All E.R. 57 (C.A.) 299
Wasp, The (1867) L.R. 1 A. & E. 367 409
Waverley Ltd v. Carnaud Metal Box Engineering plc [1994] 1 Lloyd's Rep. 38 ....281, 282
Waverley Asset Management Ltd v. Saha, 1989 SLT (Sh. Ct.) 87 162
Wavertree Sailing Ship Co. v. Love [1897] A.C. 373 597
Wayling v. Jones [1993] EGCS 153 458
Wazirstan, The [1953] 2 Lloyd's Rep. 361 589
Webb v. Webb [1994] 3 All E.R. 911 105
Weber v. Eurocard [1993] I.L.Pr. 55 (C.A. Luxembourg) 117
Weinor v. Sarl Wirion Mod'enfants (1975) ECD 1–28–B1 (Cour Superieure de Justice Lux.) 634
Wells v. Osman (1704) 2 Ld. Ray. 1044 ....381, 406
Welsh Development Agency v. Redpath Dorman Long, The Times, 4 April 1994 (C.A.) 225
Wenjiang, The [1982] 1 Lloyd's Rep. 128 286
West of England and S. Wales District Bank v. Batchelor (1882) 46 L.T. 132 452
Western Fish Products v. Pentworth D.C. [1981] 2 All E.R. 204 458
Westland v. Arab Organisation [1995] 2 All E.R. 387 575
Westminster, The (1841) 1 W. Rob. 229 28
Westport, The [1965] 1 Lloyd's Rep. 547; [1965] 2 All E.R. 167 ....340, 555
Westport, The (No. 3) [1966] 1 Lloyd's Rep. 342 71
Westport, The (No. 4) [1968] 2 Lloyd's Rep. 559 .... 36, 37
Westrup v. Great Yarmouth Steam Co. (1889) 43 Ch. D. 241 .... 43, 44
Westwood v. Bell (1815) 4 Camp. 349 452
Wexford, The (1883) 13 P.D. 10 340
Wilhelm Tell, The [1892] P. 337 ....38, 410
Willcock v. Pickfords [1979] 1 Lloyd's Rep. 244 280
Willem III, The (1871) L.R. 3 A. & E. 487 398
William and Humbert Ltd v. W. and H. Trade Marks (Jersey) Ltd [1986] 1 All E.R. 129 (H.L.) 563
William Money, The (1827) 2 Hag. Adm. 136 417
William Safford, The (1860) Lush. 69 503
Williams v. Allsup (1861) 10 C.B. (N.S.) 417 497
Williams and Glyns Bank plc v. Astro Dinamico Compania Naviera SA [1984] 1 Lloyd's Rep. 453
    (H.L.) 190, 239
Wills v. Owners of Gas Float Whitton (No. 2) [1897] A.C. 337 .... 27, 49
Winkfield, The [1902] P. 42 483
Winson, The [1982] A.C. 939; [1982] 1 Lloyd's Rep. 117 ....373, 440, 444, 449, 450
Wladyslaw Lokietek, The [1978] 2 Lloyd's Rep. 520 ....339, 516, 522, 539
World Harmony, The [1967] P. 341 ....222, 603
World Star, The [1986] 2 Lloyd's Rep. 274 330
World Star, The [1987] 1 Lloyd's Rep. 452 ....334, 337, 473
Worldwide Carriers Ltd v. Ardtran International Ltd [1983] 1 Lloyd's Rep. 61 218
Wrightson v. Macarthur and Hutchinsons Ltd [1921] 2 K.B. 807 486
Written Confirmation of an Oral Contract, Re The [1986] ECC 37 (Hanseatic C.A. Hamburg) 112

X v. Y [1990] 1 Q.B. 220; [1989] 2 Lloyd's Rep. 561; [1989] 3 All E.R. 689 ....180, 185, 306, 352
Xenos v. Wickham (1863) 14 C.B. (N.S.) 435 452
Xingcheng and Andros, The [1987] 2 Lloyd's Rep. 210 (P.C.) 219

Yanxilas, The [1982] 2 Lloyd's Rep. 445 286
Yarn Sales, Re [1994] I.L.Pr. 180 (Bundesgerichtshof) 111
Yorkshire Insurance v. Nisbet Shipping Co. Ltd [1962] 2 Q.B. 330 410
Young v. SS Scotia [1903] A.C. 501 (P.C.) 261, 263
Young Mechanic, The (1845) 30 Fed. Cas. 873 ....381, 393

Z Ltd v. A [1982] Q.B. 558 .... 299, 347, 353, 357–360, 362, 363, 494, 498
Z Bank v. Di [1994] 1 Lloyd's Rep. 656 ....362, 363
Zafiro, The [1960] P. 1 321
Zelger v. Salinitri (56/79) [1980] ECR 89; [1980] 2 CMLR 635 (ECJ) 113, 151
Zelger v. Salinitri (129/83) [1984] ECR 2397; [1985] 3 CMLR 366 (ECJ) 234
Zeta, The [1893] A.C. 468 (H.L.) 22, 33, 52
Zeus, The (1886) 6 Asp. M.L.C. 312 61
Zeus, The (1888) 13 P.D. 188 60
Zhi Jiang Kou, The [1991] LMLN 300 (C.A. NSW) 214
Zigurds, The [1932] P. 113; [1934] A.C. 209 ....473, 474, 493, 505, 506, 571
Zirje, The [1989] 1 Lloyd's Rep. 493 222
Zucker v. Tyndall Holdings plc [1993] 1 All E.R. 124 350
Zygal Dynamics plc v. NcNulty (1984) unreported (C.A.) 356

Table of Statutes

[Page numbers printed in **bold** indicate where text is reproduced]

UNITED KINGDOM

Act of 1825 for Registering of British Vessels
(6 Geo. IV, c. 110) 479
Act of 1833 (3 & 4 Wm. IV, c. 54) 479
Administration of Justice Act 1920 .... 58, 428,
610, 613, 618, 619
Pt. II 671, 677
s. 5 57
9(2)(5) 618
10 ....618, **676, 677**
12 618
(1) 622
13 618
14 618
(3) **677**
Administration of Justice Act 1956 .... 3–5, 21–23,
26, 34, 37, 40, 45, 47, 50,
51, 54, 55, 57,
67, 69–71, 73, 193, 194,
196, 197, 199,
201–203, 263, 264, 320,
428, 505, 556
Pt. I 395
V 9, 261, 656
ss. 1–8 81
s. 1 ....38, 58
(1) 38
(o) **69**, 70, 407
7(1) 42
45 ....**653, 654**
46 .... **654**
47 ....60, **654–656**
(2)(d)(e) 60
ss. 48, 49 .... **656**
s. 50 ....654, **656**
51(1) 622
Administration of Justice Act 1969—
Pt. II 666
s. 15(2) 666
Administration of Justice Act 1970—
s. 44 551
Administration of Justice Act 1982 .... 55, 622
s. 4 411
6 295
15 ....278, 281, 551, 552
53 557
Sch. 1 ....278, 281

Administration of Justice Act 1982—*cont.*
Sch. 1, Pt. I 551
Pt. IV 552
Administration of Justice Act 1985—
s. 57 223
Administration of Justice (Scotland) Act
1972—
s. 1 674
Admiralty Court Act 1840 ....3, 26, 31, 33,
34, 36, 66, 389, 427, 428
s. 3 47
4 45
6 ....26, 28, 31, 33, 67, **390**, 428
Admiralty Court Act 1861 ....3, 5, 26, 33, 35, 36,
39, 46, 389, 390, 427, 428
s. 1 428
ss. 4, 5 67
s. 6 58
7 .... 33, 428
9 428
10 ....26, 36, 407, 428
11 47
35 427
Arbitration Act 1950 ....220, 273, 275, 280,
281, 283, 284, 291, 302,
349, 564, 622, 623
Pt. II 621, 657, 658
ss. 1, 2, 3 281
s. 4 280
(1) 249, 657
ss. 6–11 281
s. 12 ....281, 290, 302, 350
(1) 290, 300
(4)(5) 283
(6) 283, 673
(a) 282
ss. 13–17, 18–20 281
s. 19A 552
20 551
21 284
(2) 284
ss. 22, 23–25 281
s. 23 ....281, 284, 553
24(2) 281, 286
26 ....291, 553, 657
27 ....**288**, 289
36(1) 621

Arbitration Act 1950—*cont.*
  s. 37(1) 622
      40(a) 621
Arbitration Act 1975 ....83, 186, 190, 273–275,
                          280, 281, 291, 621–623
  s. 1 ....245, 249, **657**
      (1) **280**
      2 .... **657**
  ss. 3–6 657
  s. 3 ....622, **657**
  ss. 4, 5 ....275, 622, **658**
  s. 6 ....622, **658**
      7 ....**658, 659**
      (1) 622
      (2)(3) 274
      35(1) 275
Arbitration Act 1979 ....273, 281, 286, 290
  s. 1(2) 284, 286
      (3)(a)(4)(5)(6)(6A)(7)(a)(b) 285
      2 284
      3(3) 281
      (7) 287
      4(3) 287
      5 ....281, 282, 290
      (1) 290
      13A 290
Arbitration Act (Northern Ireland) 1937—
  ss. 4, 16 657
  s. 2(1) 673
Arbitration (International Disputes) Act 1966   621
Banking Act 1987 ....183, 726
Bills of Sale Act 1878 ....457, 459, 472,
                          476, 479, 484, 488
  s. 4 ....457, 484
  ss. 8, 10 477
Bills of Sale Act 1882 ....457, 459, 472,
                          476, 479, 484, 488, 492
  s. 3 457
  ss. 4, 5 485
      8, 9 484
Bills of Sale Act 1890—
  s. 1 484
Carriage by Air Act 1961—
  Sch., Art. 46 217
Carriage by Air and Road Act 1979—
  Sch. 1, Art. 26 217
Carriage by Railway Act 1972—
  s. 6 217
  Sch., Art. 16 217
Carriage of Goods by Road Act 1965 ....218, 318
  s. 1 ....205, 244
      4 ....619, 675, 676
      7 622
  Sch. 80, 205
      Art. 1 80
          (5) 80
          30 217
          31 ....243, 277
          33 277
Carriage of Goods by Sea Act 1971 218,
                          219, 244, 577, 585
  s. 1(3)(6)(a) 563

Carriage of Goods by Sea Act 1971—*cont.*
  Sch., Art. III(6) 217
Carriage of Goods by Sea Act 1992 ....115, 241,
                          243, 373, 471, 492, 495,
                                          573, 599
  s. 3(1) 586
Carriage of Passengers by Road Act 1974—
  s. 5 ....619, 675, 676
Charging Orders Act 1979 ....456, 557
  s. 3(4) 494
Children Act 1989—
  Sch. 13 162
Civil Aviation Act 1949 65
Civil Aviation Act 1982 454
  s. 87 ....656, 660
Civil Jurisdiction and Judgments Act 1982   4,
                  11, 16, 17, 22, 85, 160, 162, 179,
                  180, 196, 197, 244, 296, 299, 314,
                  349, 350, 609, 610, 626, 645, 732
  Pt. I 677
      III 654
  s. 1 ....**663, 664**
      (1) 683, 733
      (2)(a)(b) 683
      (3) 683, 733
      2 .... **665**
      (2) 684
      3 ....88, **665**
      (2) 621
      (3) 669
      3A **665**
      3B **665, 666**
      4 ....**666**, 669, 671
      (2) 667
      (3) 648
      5 ....**666**, 667, 669, 671
      6 .... **666**
      7 ....**666, 667**
      9 .... **667**
      10 ....89, **161**, 667
  ss. 11, 12, 13 .... **668**
  s. 14 ....**668, 669**
      15 669
      (1) 683
      16 ....89, 159, 161, 667, **669, 670**
      (3) 162
      17 ....162, 669, **670**
      18 ....610, **670, 671**, 672
      (1) 621
      (2) 683
          (c) 672
          (e) 621
      (4) 672
      (5)(b)(d) 610
      (7) 610
      (8) 621
      19 ....**671, 672**
      (1) 610, 621
      24 ....296, 305, 330, 345, 351, 364, **672**
      25 ....180, 184, **305**, 306, 330, 345,
                          351, 364, **672, 673**
      (1) 296, 305

Civil Jurisdiction and Judgments Act
1982—*cont.*

s. 25(3) 296, 305
    (c) 283
    (4), (5) 305
    (6) 296
26 .... 196, 247, 249, 250, 268,
    271, 296, 302, 305–307,
    315, 320, **329**, 330, 331,
    338, 365, 413, 436, **673**
    (2) 302, 331
    (3) 413, 562
27 .... 296, 329, **673**, **674**
28 .... **674**
29 .... **674**, 684
30 .... 78, 589, 599, **675**
    (1) **264**
31 .... 621, **675**
    (3) 621
32 .... 615, **616**, **675**, **676**
    (1) 617
    (4) 617, 619
33 .... 616, 617, **676**
    (2) 616
34 .... 255, 324, **607**, 608, **676**
35 .... **676**, **677**
    (1)(2) 618
38 .... 619, **677**
39 .... 90, **677**, **678**
ss. 41–46 733
s. 41 .... 118, 121, **678**
    (2) **119**
    (3) 119
    (4)(5)(6) 119, 159
    (7) 119
42 .... 119–121, **678**, **679**, 680
    (2) 119
    (4)(5) 159
    (7)(8) 119
43 .... 106, 120, 121, **679**, **680**
    (1)(b)(c) 679
    (7)(a) 120
44 .... 118, 119, 121, **161**, **680**
45 .... 89, 120, **680**, **681**
46 .... 121, **681**
47 .... **681**, **682**
48 .... **682**, **683**
49 .... 167, 251, **683**
50 .... 89, 120, **683**, **684**
51 684
    (2) 683
ss. 52, 53, 54, 55 .... **684**
Sch. 1 .... **684** *et seq.*
    Title II 697
       Sections 3, 4, 5 692
    Title III 697, 703
       Section 2 704
        3 697
    Arts. 1, 2 .... **685**
    Art. 3 .... **685**, **686**
    Art. 3(2) 701
       4 .... **686**, 687, 689, 701

Civil Jurisdiction and Judgments Act
1982—*cont.*

Sch. 1, Art. 5 .... **686**, **687**, 689
    (1) 690, 702
    6 .... **687**
    (2) 703
    6a **687**
    Arts. 7, 8, 9 .... **687**, 688
    Art. 10 .... **687**, **688**, 703
    11 .... **688**
    12 .... **688**, 690
    12a **688**
    13 .... **688**, **689**
    14 .... **689**
    15 .... **689**, 690
    16 .... 686, **689**, **690**, 732
    17 .... **690**, 702, 731, 732
    Arts. 18, 19 .... **690**
    Art. 20 .... **691**, 695, 700
    Arts. 21, 22, 23, 24, 25 .... **691**
    Art. 26 .... **692**
    Arts. 27, 28 .... **692**, 693
       29, 30 .... **692**
    Art. 31 *et seq.* 697
       31 .... **693**
    Arts. 32–35 696
       32, 33, 34 .... **693**
    Art. 35 .... **694**
       36 .... **694**, 695
    Arts. 37, 38 .... **694**
       39, 40, 41, 42 .... **695**
       43, 44, 45 .... **696**
       46, 47 .... 693, **696**
       48, 49 .... **696**
       50, 51, 52, 53 .... **697**, 703
    Art. 54 .... **697**
       54a **698**, **699**
       55 .... **699**, **700**
       56 .... 699, **700**
    Arts 56, 57, 58 .... **700**
    Art. 59 .... 692, **700**, **701**
    Arts. 61, 62, 63, 64, 65, 66 .... **701**
       67, 68 .... **702**
    Protocol, Arts. I, II, III **702**
       Art. IV 701, **702**, **703**
       Arts. V, Va, Vb, Vc **703**
       Art. Vd **703**
       Art. VI 701, **703**, **704**
Sch. 3B, Art. 29(1)(2) **704**
Sch. 3C 85, 731, 732
    Title II 704
       Section 2 704
       Sections 3, 4 705
       Section 5 .... 704, 705
    Title III 705, 707, 709
    Arts. 3, 4 709
    Art. 5 .... **704**
       16 .... **704**, 707
       17 .... **705**, 707
       20 709
    Arts. 21, 22 707
    Art. 27(1) 705

Civil Jurisdiction and Judgments Act 1982—*cont.*
Sch. 3C, Art. 28 .... **705**
      54 ....**705**, 707
      54A **705**
      54B **707**
        (3) 705
      55 .... **707**
      56 ....707, **708**
      57 .... **708**
        (4) 705
      59 ....705, **709**
      60 .... **709**
      62 .... **709**
      63 .... **709**
  Protocol No. 1, Arts. I, Ia **710**
           Arts. Ib, II, III, IV, V **711**
           Arts. Va, Vb, Vd, VI **712**
  Protocol No. 2, Preamble **712**
           Arts. 1, 2, 3, 4 .... **713**
  Protocol No. 3 .... **713**
  Sch. 4 ....85, 159, 161, 613, 669,
             670, 675, 681, 731, 732
      Art. 5(2) 670
        5A 679
        16(1) 264
        (2) 679
  Sch. 5 ....159, 161–163, 670
  Sch. 6 ....610, 621, 670, 671
      para. 1 683
      paras. 5, 6, 7, 8, 9 611
      para. 10 612
  Sch. 7 ....610, 612, 670, 671
      para. 1 683
      paras. 6, 7 611
  Sch. 8 681
  Sch. 8, rr. 2(12), 4(1)(b) 679
  Sch. 9, para. 6 654
  Sch. 10 ....618, 622, 676
  Sch. 13, Pts. I, II 684
      para. 8(1) 616
        (2) 619
  Sch. 14 684
Civil Jurisdiction and Judgments Act 1991 .... 4, 11,
          16, 17, 85, 160, 179, 184,
          244, 349, 350, 645, 704
  s. 1(3) 704
  Sch. 2, para. 12 329
      para. 15 616
Civil Liability (Contribution) Act 1978 222
  s. 1(1) 411
    (5) 562
Companies Act 1948 ....321, 485
Companies Act 1985 ....106, 163, 441,
        455–459, 469, 476, 485,
        490, 495, 497
  Pt. XII 457, 472, 484–486, 488, 494
    XXIII 487
  s. 97 485
    150 457
    395(1) 485
      (2) 485, 487

Companies Act 1985—*cont.*
  s. 395(3) 487
    396 457
      (1)(2)(b)(c) 487
      (3) 486
      (9) 487
  ss. 398, 399(1) 487
  s. 400 ....457, 487
  ss. 401, 402, 403 487
    404, 405, 406 488
  s. 407(1) 487
    409 486
    410 488
    413 487
    414 486
    415(2)(a) 488
  ss. 692, 695(1)(2) 176
    703A, 703L 487
  s. 726 301
Companies Act 1989 ....441, 455, 457, 458,
        485, 486, 490, 495, 497
  ss. 92–107 486
    92, 105 487
  s. 106 ....486, 487
    200 162
    398(1) 486
  Sch. 15 487
Consular Relations Act 1968 ....256, 266
  ss. 4, 5 265
  s. 16 256
Consumer Arbitration Agreements Act 1988 . 273
Consumer Protection Act—
  s. 6 223
  Sch. 1 223
Contempt of Court Act 1981—
  s. 16 671
Continental Shelf Act 1964—
  s. 3 ....163, 174
Contracts (Applicable Law) Act 1990 ....215, 240,
      277, 561, 565, 570, 574, 579, 581,
      583, **714** *et seq.*
  s. 1 .... **714**
    2 .... **714**
    (1), (2) 582
    (3) 574, 582
    3 .... **715**
    4 ....**715**, 716
    5 .... **715**
    6 .... **715**
  ss. 7, 8, 9 .... **716**
  Sch. 1, Art. 1 .... **716**
      (2)(d) 565
    2 .... **717**
    Arts. 3–6 719
    Art. 3 ....**717**, 718
      (3) 565
    4 .... **717**
    5 ....**718**, 719
      (2) 719
    6 .... **718**
    7 .... **719**
      (1) 565, 721

Contracts (Applicable Law) Act 1990—*cont.*
Sch. 1, Art. 7(2) 565
        8 .... 717, **719**
        9 .... 717, **719**, 720
       10 .... **719**
          (1)(c) 572
          (e) 721
       11 ....716, 717, **720**
       12 .... 719, **720**
       13 .... **720**
       14 .... 717, **720**
          (1)(2) 573
    Arts. 15, 16, 17 .... **720**
       18, 19, 21 .... **721**
    Art. 22 .... **721**, 723
      23 .... **721**, 723
    Arts. 24, 25, 26 .... **722**, 723
    Art. 27 .... **722**, 723
       (2) 721, 723
      28 .... **722**
      29 .... **722**
      30 .... **723**, 727
    Arts. 31, 32, 33 .... **723**
    Protocol **723**
Sch. 2 .... 581, **723–724**
Sch. 3 .... 582, **724–727**
Sch. 4 715
County Courts Act 1984—
  ss. 26–31 9
  s. 26 191
    27(1)(2) 191, 211
      (3) 9
      (6) 9, 191, 211
    28(3)(4) 211
      (9)(10) 322
  ss. 29, 30 191
County Courts Admiralty Jurisdiction Amendment Act 1869—
  s. 2 .... 58, 63
Court of Exchequer (Scotland) Act 1856—
  s. 13 671
Courts and Legal Services Act 1990 281
  s. 102 290
  Sch. 18 9
Criminal Justice Act 1988—
  Pt. VI 183, 671, 732
Criminal Justice (Scotland) Act 1987—
  Pt. I 671
Crown Proceedings Act 1947 ....260, 262, 263
  ss. 5–7 261
    7(3), 17(1) 262
  s. 29(1) **261**, 326
    (2) 261
    30(1) 221
    38(2) 261, **262**, 655, 663
    40(1) 260
Crown Proceedings (Armed Forces) Act 1987 260
Customs and Excise Management Act 1979—
  ss. 28(2), 49, 53, 66(2), 67 49

Customs and Excise Management Act 1979—*cont.*
  ss. 68(5), 74, 76 48
  s. 78(4) 49
    88 48
  ss. 89, 90, 141 49
  s. 142 .... 48, 49
  Sch. 3 48
Cyprus Act 1960—
  s. 2(1) 716
Dangerous Vessels Act 1985—
  s. 2 545
Diplomatic Privileges Act 1964 256
Diseases of Animals Act 1950—
  s. 75(2) 42, 656
Drug Trafficking Act 1994 671
Drug Trafficking Offences Act 1986 .... 183, 732
Employers' Liability (Defective Equipment) Act 1969 55
Employment Protection (Consolidation) Act 1978—
  s. 153(3) 562
Evidence (Foreign, Dominion and Colonial Documents) Act 1933 573
Evidence (Proceedings in Other Jurisdictions) Act 1975 272
Factors Act 1889 481
  s. 2 .... 481, 496
  ss. 8, 9 ....473, 481, 496
  s. 10 473
Family Law Act 1986—
  Pt. I 671
Fatal Accidents Act 1846 34
Fatal Accidents Act 1976 .... 34, 55, 223, 562, 564
Financial Services Act 1986 .... 183, 732
  s. 188 163
Foreign Judgments (Reciprocal Enforcement) Act 1933 ....15, 301, 542, 610, 613, 617–619
  Pt. I 618, 671, 675, 676
  ss. 1(1)(2)(10), 2A 618
  s. 4(1)(a)(b)(3)(b) 619
    10A 618, 622, 623
Foreign Limitation Periods Act 1984 .... 213, 215, 216, 561, 570
  s. 1 .... 215, 570
    2 215
    (1), (2) 570
    (3) 215, 570
    3 .... 617, 619
    4(3) 570
    7 215
Friendly Societies Act 1992—
  s. 101 583
      (1)(a), (2)(a) 715
  Sch. 20 .... 583, 715
Harbours, Docks and Piers Clauses Act 1847—
  ss. 44, 47, 56 453
  s. 74 44
Hotel Proprietors Act 1956—
  s. 2 446

Hovercraft Act 1968—
  s. 1 64
    (1)(h) 19
    2 .... 19, 64
    (2) 27, 31, 395, 398
    (3) 31, 261, 395, 663
Immigration Act 1971—
  s. 25(6) 48
Immigration (Carriers' Liability) Act 1987 183,
                                                   732
Inferior Courts Judgments Extension Act
  1882 610
Insolvency Act 1985—
  Sch. 10 671
Insolvency Act 1986 ....416, 441, 454
  s. 11(1)(b) 375
    (3)(c)(d) 376
    15(1)–(3)(4)(5) 376
  ss. 29(2), 73 375
  s. 112 ....321, 375, 443
    125 321
    126 ....321, 375, 443
    127 375
    128 ....321, 375, 443
    130 321
      (2) 375, 443
    183 321
    236 444
  ss. 238–247 375
  s. 238 564
    246 ....375, 442
    248 376
    283 411
    285 ....321, 376, 443
      (1)(2)(3)(4) 376, 416
    346 321
      (1) 376
    426 671
Insurance Companies Act 1982—
  s. 94B 583
  Sch. 3A 583, 714
International Transport Conventions Act
  1983 217
  s. 6 ....619, 675, 676
Interpretation Act 1968—
  s. 17(2)(b) 477
Interpretation Act 1978—
  s. 12(1) 684
    21(1) 715
Judgment Extension Act 1868 ....610, 613
Judgments Act 1838 551
Latent Damage Act 1986 ....218, 223
Law of Property Act 1925—
  s. 136(1) 466, 493, 494
Law Reform (Limitation of Actions) Act
  1954—
  s. 5(1), (2) 221
Law Reform (Miscellaneous Provisions) Act
  1934 ....55, 551
  s. 1(1) 411
Law Reform (Miscellaneous Provisions)
  (Scotland) Act 1985 674

Limitation Act 1939 218
Limitation Act 1980 ....174, 175,
                              218–220, 222, 225, 287
  s. 2 223
    3 ....213, 223
  ss. 4A, 5 223
  s. 7 ....223, 288
  ss. 8, 9 223
  s. 10 222
    11 ....218, 223
    11A 223
    12 ....218, 223
    13 223
  ss. 14, 14A 218, 223
  s. 14B 218
  ss. 15, 16 222
  s. 17 213
    20 ....222, 223
    21 222
    22 223
    23 222
    24 ....223, 229
      (2) 229
    25 213
  ss. 28–32, 32A 223
  s. 33 ....218, 223
    34(1)(2)(3)(4)(5) 288
    35 ....175, 215, 218, 224
    36(1) 223, 226
      (2) 223
    39 ....218, 288
    40(1) 224
  Sch. 2, para. 9(2) 224
Limitation Amendment Act 1980 229
  s. 8 224
    9 218
      (2) 223
Magistrates' Court Act 1980—
  s. 11 666
Maintenance and Affiliation Orders Act
  (Northern Ireland) 1966—
  s. 11A 667
Maintenance Orders Act 1950—
  Pt. II 671
  s. 15(1)(a) 670
    16 671
Maintenance Orders Act 1958—
  s. 2A 667
Maintenance Orders (Reciprocal Enforcement)
  Act 1972—
  Pt. I 671
Marine Insurance Act 1906 448
  s. 4 267
    53(2) **452**, 496
    66(2) **72**
    79 410
Marine Insurance (Gambling Policies) Act
  1909 267
Maritime Conventions Act 1911 ....35, 219,
                                     221, 222, 428
  s. 1 593
  ss. 2, 3(2) 411

Maritime Conventions Act 1911—*cont.*
s. 5 ....**33**, 34, 55
  7 598
  8 ....214, 219, 221
Merchant Seaman Act 1844—
s. 16 ....38, 390, 407
Merchant Shipping Act 1854 ....390, 479, 515
  s. 2 38
  191 .... 38, 407
  458 .... 29, 31
Merchant Shipping Act 1889 390
  s. 1 39
Merchant Shipping Acts 1894–1940 262
Merchant Shipping Acts 1894–1981 70
Merchant Shipping Acts 1894–1994 69
Merchant Shipping Act 1894 ....30, 38, 49, 64,
                  448, 476, 479, 480
  Pt. IX 27, 49, 399
  s. 3 477
    24(1) 56
    30 ....46, 73, 298
    55 73
    165 656
    167(1) 38
    (2) **39**
  ss. 418, 421(1)(2) 183, 735
  s. 449(1)(2) 49
  ss. 493, 494–496 ....449, 450
  s. 494 452
  ss. 497, 498 450
  s. 499 ....450, 452
    504 528
    510 27
    (1) 399
    513(1)(2) 43
    521 218
  ss. 530, 531 453
  s. 544 ....29, 65, 66, 397, 502
    (2) 30
    545 66
    546 ....28, **30**, 31, 65, 66, 397
  ss. 552, 554 415
  s. 556 65
  ss. 567(2), 568(1) 42
    650, 651 453
  s. 683(1)(2) 218
    741 ....261, 262
    742 ....31, 36, 395
Merchant Shipping Act 1906 477
  s. 72 50
    80 ....261, 262
Merchant Shipping Act 1970 .... 69, 70
  ss. 7–18 35
  s. 7 38
    12 36
    14 70
    16 ....28, 36
    18 ....36, 38, 39
    26 ....36, 70
    43 38
  ss. 62–64 70
  s. 62 36

Merchant Shipping Act 1970—*cont.*
  s. 67 70
    100(3) 38
  Sch. 3, para. 4 38
Merchant Shipping Act 1974 ....35, 53, 54, 81,
            84, 219, 521, 522, 540
  s. 4 ....183, 735, 736
    (1)(2) 84
    (12)(b) 736
    4A 543
    6(2) 736
    (4) 619
    7 219
  Sch. 1 543
Merchant Shipping Act 1979 ....24, 277, 339,
           414, 509, 521, 529–531,
           533, 542, 735, 744
  ss. 4(8)–(9A), 8, 13(3) 542
  s. 14 244
    17 ....244, 527
    (4) 527
    18 527
    19 545
  ss. 20, 20A 83
  s. 21 ....183, 593, 735
    (2) 593
    22 593
    35(2) 528
    37(1) 35
    41 395
    47 593
    50(4) 263
  Sch. 3 79
    Art. 15 217
  Sch. 4 738
    Pt. I 522
    II 522, 528
      para. 4 528
      para. 8(1) 529
      para. 9 519
      para. 10 319
  Sch. 5, Pt. I 545
    para. 5 261
Merchant Shipping Act 1983 477
Merchant Shipping Act 1988 ....28, 30,
           53, 476, 477, 522
  s. 30A 346, 453
    46 ....35, 38
    47 477
  Sch. 1, para. 32 73
  Sch. 4, Pts. I, II 84
  Sch. 5, para. 3 29
Merchant Shipping Act 1995 ....4, 20, 27,
    29, 54, 64, 70, 73, 74, 106, 219,
    222, 395, 397, 399, 414, 475–477,
    482, 484, 485, 497, 506, 509, 533,
    540, 543, 656, 660, 661, 663, 735
  Pt. I 472, 600
    II 472, 477, 479, 488
    VI 30, 81, 84, 332, 336, 521, 522, 541, 542
    Chap. III 540, 660
    IV 540

Merchant Shipping Act 1995—*cont.*
Pt. VI, Chap. VI 660
    VII 263, 521, 541, 543–545
        Chap. III 53
    IX 30
        Chap. 1 410
            2 49
s. 1 30
    (1) 265
ss. 2, 3, 4(3)(4) 48
s. 15(1) 477
    16(1) 489
ss. 17–19 339
s. 17(7) 478, 479, 482, 492, 562, 567
    24(1) 56
ss. 30–41 ....35, 38
s. 30(1) 38
    34(1) 557
        (c) 410
    35 36
    37 70
    39 ....28, 36, 403, 410
    41 ....36, 38, **39**, 403
    45 70
    47 38
ss. 73–75 70
s. 85 ....593, 656, 663
    86 593
    87(1)(3) 49
    95 346
        (1) 453
    128 83
    146 453
    149 .... 261, 262
    153 .... 53, 540
    154 53
    157 .... 53, 540
        (3) 541
    158(1)(2) **540**
        (4) 541
        (7) **540**
        (8) 53, **541**
ss. 159, 160 541
s. 162 219
    165 53
        (3) 541
    166(2) 84
        (4) 542, 619, 675
    167 261
        (1) 263
ss. 169, 175(8)(10) 542
s. 176 543
        (3) 543
    177(4) 619, 676
    178 219
    183(1) 244
    185 244
        (1) 527
        (4) 528
    186 ....518, 520, 527
ss. 187–189 221
s. 187 ....221, 593

Merchant Shipping Act 1995—*cont.*
s. 188 ....221, 593
    190 ....214, 219, **221**
    191 545
    192 ....221, 261
ss. 208, 209 453
s. 224 ....66, 219, 244, 473, 655, 660
    226 663
        (3) 415
    234(6) 43
    236 50
ss. 239(1), 274L 218
s. 249(3) 42
    250(2) 42
ss. 252, 253 453
s. 255 399
    275 218
    307 593
    308 ....260, 261, 477
        (1)(3) 262
    309 477
    311 395
    313(1) 36, 38, 262, 395
Sch. 1 472
    para. 1 489
        (1) 478, 491
        (2) 478, 479, 491
    paras. 2–13 478
    para. 2 73
        (1)(2)–(4) 479
    paras. 3–5 479
    para. 4(4) 48
        5 30
        6 ....46, 73, 298
        7 489
            (2) 478
        8 490
        10 483
Sch. 2, para. 8(2) 490
Sch. 3, para. 1 48
        3(3) 453
        5(1)(4)(5) 48
Sch. 4 ....53, 339
Sch. 5 543
Sch. 6 180
    Art. 15 217
Sch. 7 ....522, 562
    Pt. II 528
        para. 4 528
        para. 8(2) 517
        para. 9 ....419, 509, 519
    Art. 13(2) 415
Sch. 8, Pt. II, para. 10 319
Sch. 11 ....219, 222, 417, 473
    para. 1 31
        2 ....29, 31
        5 502
Sch. 13, para. 59 ....35, 53
        (2) 66
        74 545

Merchant Shipping (Liability of Shipowners and Others) Act 1900—

s. 2 545

Merchant Shipping (Liability of Shipowners and Others) Act 1958 .... 339, 522

s. 5 339

Merchant Shipping (Load Lines) Act 1967—

s. 3(4) 453

Merchant Shipping (Oil Pollution) Act 1971 . 24, 35, 53, 54, 81, 219, 332, 336, 395, 521, 522, 540

s. 1 .... 53, 183, 735, 736, 738

1A 53

4 .... 53, 54

(3) 541

(7)(8)(12) 54

5 540

(3) 541

(7) 53

ss. 6(1), 7 541

s. 9 219

12 53

(3) 541

13(2) 732

(3) 619

(4) 83

14 261

Merchant Shipping (Registration etc.) Act 1993 .... 346, 472, 476, 477, 479, 480, 488, 600

s. 7(7) 482, 492

Sch. 1, para. 2 73

(6) 73

6 .... 46, 298

Sch. 2, para. 3 261

Sch. 4 49

para. 4(5) 593

11(2)(a)(l) 49

Sch. 5 415

Merchant Shipping (Salvage and Pollution) Act 1944 502

Merchant Shipping (Salvage and Pollution) Act 1994 .... 26, 27, 29, 30, 53, 54, 56, 64, 81, 219, 260, 395, 397, 399, 435, 598

s. 1 .... 66, 244

(6) 31, 64, 473

ss. 3, 4 83

s. 5 84

Sch. 1 222

Pt. II, para. 2 31

Sch. 2 473

para. 1 31

(2) 66, 428

3 326

4 64

5 528

6 .... 64, 427

(3) 66

para. 7 .... 64, 191, 211

28(2) 191

Merchant Shipping (Stevedores and Trimmers) Act 1911 428

Mineral Workings (Offshore Installation) Act 1971 174

Nuclear Installations Act 1965 .... 54, 183, 732

s. 13 84

14 .... 31, 263

17(1) 84

(4) 619, 675, 676

Oath and Evidence (Overseas Authorities and Countries) Act 1963—

s. 5 573

Occupiers' Liability Act 1957 55

Oil and Gas (Enterprise) Act 1982 174

Pilotage Act 1913—

s. 15(1) 402

Pilotage Act 1983—

s. 35 402

Pilotage Act 1987 .... 520, 521, 543

s. 10(9) 67

16 402

22(1)–(3) 543

(3)(4) 544

(6) **544**

Piracy Act 1850—

s. 5 49

Post Office Act 1969—

ss. 6(5), 29, 30 262

Prescription and Limitation (Scotland) Act 1973—

s. 23A 570

Prevention of Oil Pollution Act 1971—

s. 20 453

24 .... 261, 262

Private International Law (Miscellaneous Provisions) Act 1995 .... 561, 564, 565, 569, 570, 572, 574, 591, 592

s. 1 551

9(2) 562, 574

11 .... **591**, 592

12 .... **592**

14(2) 592

(3) 562

(4) 592

Pt. III, paras. 9, 10, 11 .... **763**

12, 13, 14 .... **764**

para. 15 .... **765**

Pt. IV, paras. 16, 17, 18, 19 .... **765**

Protection of Trading Interests Act 1980 ... 163, 271, 272, 563, 615, 618, 619

s. 1 271

ss. 2, 3(2), 4 272

s. 5(1) 619, 620

(2) 620

(c) 620

(3) 620, 677

(4)(5) 620

6 .... 620, 677

7 .... 619, 677

(1A) **677**

8(5) 271

Protection of Wrecks Act 1973 49
Public Authorities Protection Act 1893 383
Responsibility of Shipowners Act 1733 515
Sale of Goods Act 1893—
  s. 25 496
Sale of Goods Act 1979 ....200, 476, 481, 508
  s. 21 .... 459, 481
  ss. 23–25 481
    24, 25 ....461, 473, 496, 507
  s. 39 .... 439, 447
    41 ....372, 458, 496
    43 372
    47 .... 473, 497
    48 ....439, 447, 497
    52 552
Sale of Goods (Amendment) Act 1995 476
Sheriff Courts (Scotland) Act 1907 654
Shipping and Trading Interests (Protection)
  Act 1995 ....271, 563
Shipping Contracts and Commercial Docu-
  ments Act 1964 271
Slave Trade Act 1824—
  s. 4 48
Social Security Act 1975 .... 183, 732
Social Security (Consequential Provisions)
  Act 1992—
  Sch. 2 162
Solicitors Act 1860—
  s. 28 496
Solicitors Act 1932—
  s. 69 496
Solicitors Act 1957—
  s. 72 496
Solicitors Act 1974 ....444, 509, 510
  s. 73 496
    81 742
State Immunity Act 1978 ....256, 257 et seq., 621
  s. 1(1) 257
  ss. 2–11 ....257, 621
  s. 2 ....258, 260, 675
    (4)(5) 258
    3 258
    (2) 258
    3(3) 258, 259
  ss. 4, 5, 6, 7 258
  s. 8 259
    9 258
    10 ....259, 260
    (1)(2) 259
    (3) 259, 263
    (4) 259
    (5) 259, 263
    (6) 260
    11 ....259, 260, 675
    12 ....259, 675
    (7) 259
    13 ....257, 675
    (2) 326
    (4) 258, 259, 326, 327
    (5) 258
    14 257
    (3)(4) 675

State Immunity Act 1978—cont.
  s. 17(1) 259
  ss. 18, 19 620
Statute Law (Repeals) Act 1993 452
  Sch. 1, Pt. XV, Group 6 450
Supreme Court Act 1981 .... 4, 9, 12, 17, 19,
    22, 23, 34, 40, 41, 45, 47, 51, 57,
    69, 74, 82, 193, 196, 197, 201,
    202, 204, 205, 261–264, 295, 315,
    316, 320, 321, 346, 350, 367, 378,
    395, 428, 475, 483, 492, 614
  s. 5 14
    6(i)(b) 9
  ss. 20–23 ....265, 663
    20–24 ....9, 261
  s. 20 ....9, 10, 19, 20,
    24, 25, 70, 72, 81, 171,
    313, 391,
    427, 435, 506, 567, 601,
    659–661
    (1) 19, 25
    (a) 19
    (b) 19, 69, 70, 73, 74
    (c) 20, 21, 38, 51, 74,
      193–195, 205, 378, 427,
      432, 434, 435, 437
    (d) 19, 20, 23, 427, 434, 437
    (e)–(r) 197, 211, 378, 432
    (2)–(6) 19
    (2) 11, 30, 50, 57, 70, 495
    (a)–(c) 11, 196, 378
    (a) 45, 193, 203, 427,
      429, 431, 432, 437, 661
    (b) 46, 193, 203, 427,
      429, 431, 432, 437, 661
    (c) 47, 193, 203, 427,
      429, 431, 432, 437, 456,
      661
    (d)–(r) 50, 191
    (d) 11, 50, 57, 73, 194, 437, 567
    (e)–(r) 193–196, 203, 204,
      379, 401, 427, 429–432,
      434, 437, 661
  s. 20(2)(e)–(s) 11
    (e) 21, 52, 57, 58
    (f) 32, 52, **55**
    (g) 56–59, 65
    (h) 56, 58, 59, 62, 63, 65, 431
    (j) 19, 64, 65, 427, 429, 431
    (k) 19, 66
    (l) 19, 67
    (m)(n) 67, 69, 429
    (o) 37, 69, 407, 562
    (p) 67, 71
    (q) 71, 72
    (r) 72, 431, 494
    (s) 48, 49, 193, 196,
      203, 378, 427, 429, 431, 432, 437,
      661
    (3) 70
    (a) 69, 70, 73
    (b) 73

Supreme Court Act 1981—*cont.*

s. 20(3)(c) 66, 74, 530
    (l) 46
    (4) 46
    (5) 53
      (a)(b) 35
    (6) 29, 30, 64, 66
      (a) 66
    (7) **20**, 69, 70, 500
      (b) 64
      (c) 47, 456, 567
ss. 21–23 69
  21–24 9
s. 21 ....10, 11, 21, 50, 68, 501, 567, 601, **661**
    (1) 11, **171**, 193, 506
      (a)(b)(c)(e)–(r)(s) 195
    (2) 24, **193**, 195, 196, 205,
        378, 434, 435, 456, 495
      (c) 500
    (3) 9, **10**, 19, 20, 24,
        38, 66, 69, 193, **194**, 195,
        203–205, 378, 429, 568
    (4) 24, 25, 50, 51, 57, 63,
        68, 72, **193**, 195, 202–205, 322,
        332, 378, 379, 387, 394, 429, 430,
        433–435, 506, 737
      (a) 57
      (b) 435
    (6) 554
    (7) 437
      (c) 500
    (8) 195, 199, 204, 207, 322,
        323, 332, 387, 429, 430
  22 ....73, 81, 83, 171, 180, 188, 316, **661**, **662**
    (2) 663
    (5) 533
  23 ....81, 84, **264**, **662**
  24 ....**663**
    (1) 66, 67, 264, 395
    (2) 326
      (a) 69, 265
      (c) **261**
  31(3) 347
ss. 32, 32A 299
  33–35 296
  33(1), 35 298
s. 35A(1) **551**
    (2) 551
    (3) 551, 552
  37 ....283, 296, 298, 303
    (1) 297, 348, 557
    (3) 299, **348**, 352
  40 557
  49 ....351, 549
    (3) 98
ss. 61–65 12
s. 61(3)(5) 23
  62(2) 9
  64 ....9, 73
  65 73
  72 296
  138 557

Supreme Court Act 1981—*cont.*

s. 140 671
  148 285
  152(i) 64
Sch. 1 12
Sch. 5 ....19, 64
Supreme Court of Judicature Act 1873 ....12, 13,
    22, 295, 351
Supreme Court of Judicature Act 1875 ....12, 13,
    22, 351
Supreme Court of Judicature (Consolidation)
  Act 1925 ....3, 34, 47, 71, 295, 428, 556
s. 22 ....55, 72
    (1)(a)(i) 45, 67
      (iii)–(iv) 33
      (vii) 38, 67
      (ix) 47
      (x) 67
      (xii) 57, 58
ss. 36, 37, 42 351
s. 43 ....351, 549
  45 298
Territorial Sea Act 1987 174
Third Party (Rights Against Insurers) Act
  1930 411
Torts (Interference with Goods) Act 1977—
  s. 4 299
  ss. 12, 13 439
Trade Union and Employment Rights Act
  1993 267
Trade Union and Labour Relations (Consolidation) Act 1992—
  s. 219(1) **266**
    221(2) 297
  ss. 222–226, 234A, 244(1)(2)(3)(4) 267
Unfair Contract Terms Act 1977—
  s. 27 562
Wrecks and Salvage Act 1846—
  s. 19 31

AUSTRALIA
Sea Carriage of Goods Act 1924—
  s. 9 ....**244**
Trade Practices Act—
  s. 81(1A) 620

BELGIUM
Civil Code—
  Art. 15 ....102, 685
Judicial Code—
  Art. 638 685

DENMARK
Law of Civil Procedure
  Art. 246(2)(3) 685
    248 102
  Arts. 646–653 706
Statute on Maritime Law—
  para. 169 723

FRANCE
Civil Code—
  Arts. 14, 15 ....102, 685

GERMANY
Code of Civil Procedure—
  Art. 23 .... 102, 685
  Arts. 68, 72, 73, 74 .... 156, 703

GREECE
Code of Civil Procedure—
  Art. 40 .... 102, 685

ICELAND
Law on Arrest and Injunction—
  Chap. III 707

ITALY
Code of Civil Procedure 102
  Arts. 2, 4 686

LUXEMBOURG
Civil Code—
  Arts. 14, 15 .... 102, 686

NETHERLANDS
Code of Civil Prodecure—
  Art. 126(3) 686
  127 .... 102, 686

NEW ZEALAND
Ship Registration Act 1992—
  s. 70 492

PORTUGAL
Code of Civil Procedure—
  Arts. 65(1)(c)(2), 65A(c) 686
  Art. 165 102
Code of Labour Procedure—
  Art. 11 686

SINGAPORE
Rules of Supreme Court 211

SOUTH AFRICA
Admiralty Jurisdiction Regulation Act
  1983—
  s. 5(3) 330

UNITED STATES OF AMERICA
Carriage of Goods by Sea Act 245
Clayton Act 620
Federal Arbitration Act—
  9 USC 14, 201–08, s. 8 330
Limitation of Liability Act 537

Table of Statutory Instruments

[Page numbers printed in **bold** indicate where text is reproduced]

Admiralty Rules 1859—

r. 10 265

Arbitration (Foreign Awards) Order 1984 (SI 1984 No. 1168) 622

Carriage of Passengers and their Luggage by Sea (Domestic Carriage) Order 1987 (S.I. 1987 No. 670) 80

Child Support Act 1991 (Consequential Amendments) Order 1993 (SI 1993 No. 785) 35

Civil Courts Order 1983 (SI 713 No. 1983) .. 191

Civil Jurisdiction and Judgments Act 1982 (Amendment) Order 1993 (SI 1993 No. 603) 85, 161

Civil Jurisdiction and Judgments (Authentic Instruments and Court Settlements) Order 1993 (SI 1993 No. 604) 626, 627

Collision Regulations and Distress Signals Order 1977 (SI 1977 No. 682) 594

Contracts (Applicable Law) Act 1990 (Amendment) Order 1994 (SI 1994 No. 1900) 561, 581, 714

County Court Rules 1981 (SI 1981 No. 1687)—

Ord. 40 .... 191, 211, 554

r. 13 .... 211, 338

County Court Remedies (Amendment) Regulations 1995 (SI 1995 No. 206) 347

County Courts (Northern Ireland) Order 1980—

Arts. 46, 48(f) 674

Hovercraft (Application of Enactments) Order 1972 (SI 1972 No. 971) 19

Art. 8 .... 27, 64

Judgment Debts (Rate of Interest) Order 1993 (SI 1993 No. 564) 551

Merchant Shipping (Distress Signals and Prevention of Collision) Regulations 1989 (SI 1989 No. 1798) 593

Merchant Shipping (MOD Commercially Managed Ships) Order 1992 (SI 1992 No. 1293) 261

Merchant Shipping (MOD Yachts) Order 1992 (SI 1992 No. 1294) 261

Merchant Shipping (Registration of Ships) Regulations 1993 (SI 1993 No. 3138) 477, 506, 600

reg. 1 .... 477, 479

2 478

3 .... 477, 479, 489

5 478

6 479

regs. 7–13, 14, 15, 17 477

reg. 59 490

regs. 64–70 478

reg. 88 477

reg. 91 .... 478, 479, 489

Merchant Shipping (Salvage and Pollution) Act 1994 (Commencement No. 1) Order 1994 (SI 1994 No. 1988) 30

Merchant Shipping (Salvage and Pollution) Act 1994 (Commencement No. 2) Order 1994 (SI 1994 No. 2971) 30

Merchant Shipping (Tonnage) Regulations 1982 (SI 1982 No. 841) 522

Procedural Rules of The United Kingdom and Ireland 102

Rules of The Supreme Court 1883—

Ord. V, r. 16 265

Rules of The Supreme Court 1965 (SI 1965 No. 1776) 296, 309

Ord. 2, r. 1 .... 174, 176, 225, 227, **729**

3, r. 2(5) 730

5 .... 175, 177, 214, 227

5, rr. 1, 2 173

6, rr. 1, 2 173

r. 6 181

7 .... 180, 736

(1) 737

7A 173, 740

(3)(a) 740

8 .... 174, 181, 227, **729**, **730**

(1)(a) 207

8 300

10 .... 174, 187, 382

r. 1 .... 175, **730**

(1) 733

(3) 175

(4) 175, 323, 733, 739, 743

(5) 323, 733, 739

(6) 733

Rules of The Supreme Court 1965—*cont.*

Ord. 10, r. 3 .... **731**
     5 .... 175, 176
    11 ....174, 179, 181,
        183, 185, 188, 189, 269,
        306, 532, 581, 729
    r. 1 ....77, 148, 188, 350, **731–733**, 737
      (1) 181, **182**, **183**, 531, 731, 733
        (a) 184
        (b) 184, 185
        (c) 184, 188, 733
        (d) 184
          (iii) 565, 566
        (e) 181, 184
        (f)(iii) 597
        (i) 165
        (t) 184
      (2) 162, 179, 531, 731, 737
      (3) 186
      (4) 181
    rr. 2, 3 737
    r. 4 .... **733**
      (1) 737
      (2) 181, 737
      (4) 737
    rr. 5–8 186
    r. 5 .... **733**, **734**
      (1)–(3) 187
      (5), (6) 187
      6 .... 187, 733
      7 ....733, 734
      8 187
      9 733
      11(4) 180
    12 .... 177, 736
    r. 5 .... 176, 227
      6 227
      (1) 176, 734
      (2) 176
      7 ....176, 730, 734
      8 ......175, 177, 189, 227, 239, **734**, **735**
      (1) 181
      (6) 177, 189
      (7) 189
      8A 174
      12(10) 177
    13 743
    r. 1 177
      7 211
    14 ....177, 280, 289 298
    r. 1(2) 177
      (c) 211
    rr. 3, 4 177
    15 553
    r. 1(5) 190
    rr. 6–8 175
    r. 6 224
      (6)(e) 225
      7 225
    16 553
    18, r. 8 213
      19(1)(b) (d) 267

Rules of The Supreme Court 1965—*cont.*

Ord. 18, r. 22 520
      103 227
    19 .... 177, 743
    r. 1 743
    20 .... 175, 224
    r. 1 ....175, 225, 739
      (2) 739
      (3)(c) 175
      2 225
    rr. 3(1), 4 175
    r. 5 ....175, 220, 225
      (1), (2), (3) 225
      (5) 224
      8 175
    21, r. 1 735
    22 415
    rr. 10, 11, 13 745
    23 301
    r. 1 646
    24 360
    25 ....227, 746, 747
    26 360
    28, r. 7 305
    29 ....268, 296, 297, 300
    r. 1 349
    rr. 2, 3 298
    r. 4 .... 360, 554
      7A 298
      8A 296
    rr. 9, 17 299
    31 296
    32, rr. 1–6 300
    38, r. 13 296
      21 746
    45, r. 1 557
      4 558
      5 ....557, 558
      6 229
      13 558
    46 558
    47 200
    r. 1 .... 275, 623
      (1) 648
      5 557
    Ords. 49, 50, 51, 52 557
    Ord. 65, rr. 1, 2 176
    r. 3 .... 176, 187
      4 733
      10 740
    71 ....618, 619, 645
    r. 1 618
    rr. 30, 32 612
    r. 37 611
      (3) 612
      38 612
    73 ....285, 290, 553
    r. 3 287
      7 ....553, 622
      10 553
    74 171
    r. 1 .... 23, 73

Rules of The Supreme Court 1965—*cont.*
Ord. 75 .... 171, 179, 188, 189, 306, 379,
382, 529, 531, 532, 540,
545
r. 1 .... **735**
2 ....179, 188, 530, **735**
(1) 23, 74, 182, **183**, 731
(a) 736, 743
(b) 23, 736
(c) 23, 737
A 23, **736**
(1), (3) 336
3 .... 173, 205, 211, 227, **736**
(3) 530
(4) 177, 180
(6) 178, 205, 211
4 ....72, 74, 77,
179, 188, 531, 729, **736**,
737
(1) 188, 530
(c) 188
(2) 188
(4) 179
5 ....69, 205, 300, 322, 332, **737**, **738**
(2) 332
(3) 325
(4) 322
(5) 266, 326
(6) 332
(9) 322
(d) 266
6 ....342, 735, **738**
(1), (1A), (2) 325
A 529
7 .... 325, 337, 341, **738**, **739**
8 ....205, 208, **739**, 743
(1) 398, 436
(2) 205, 208, 323, 436
(3) 323, 334
(3A) 323, 743
(4) 325, 742
9 .... **739**
10 .... 205, 300, 322, **739**, **740**
(3) 334
(5) 398
11 ....205, 208, **740**
(1) 332
(2) 332
(b) 208
12 .... 333, 335, 554, **740**, **741**
(3) 333
13 .... 344, 415, **741**

Rules of The Supreme Court 1965—*cont.*
Ord. 75, r. 13(1) 338
(3) 338, 341
(4) 338
(7), (8) 334
14 ....735, **741**
(1) 341
15 ....325, 341, **742**
16 .... **742**
(1), (2), (3), (4) 342
17 .... 336, **742**
(3), (4) 730
18 171
21 ....**742**, **743**
(1), (2) 324, 325
(7) 211
22 ....554, **743**, **744**
23 .... 340, 554
(1) 555
A(2), (3) 334
24 415
(2), (3) 745
25 227
37 ....530, **744**
(5) 530
A 529, 738, **744**, **745**
38 ....744, **745**, **746**
(1)–(4), (5)–(9) 530
39 ....531, 744, **746**
(1) 531
40 ....531, 744, **746**, **747**
(2) 531
76 .... 182, 732
App. A, Form 1 736
14 .... 730, 736
B, Forms 1, 2, 2B 736
Form 3 737
Forms 5, 5A 738
Form 6 739
Forms 7, 9 741
Forms 10, 11 742
Form 15 737
Rules of the Supreme Court (Amendment)
1993 (SI 1993 No. 2133) 207
Safety (Collision Regulations and Distress
Signals) Regulations 1979 (SI 1979 No.
1659) 594
State Immunity (Merchant Shipping) (USSR)
Order 1978 (SI 1978 No. 1524) 327

Table of Conventions

[Page numbers printed in **bold** indicate where text is reproduced]

Accession Convention 1978 .... 111, 139, 143,
    153, 663, 683, 704
  Art. 37 665
    39 664
    41 665
Accession Convention 1982 .... 664, 683, 704
  Art. 15 664
    17 665
Accession Convention 1985 158
Accession Convention 1989 .... 664, 683
  Title VI 704
  Art. 29 .... **704**
    32 664
    34 665
Arrest Convention 1952 (Convention relating
  to the Arrest of Sea-Going Ships) 3–5, 15,
    19, 34, 47, 50, 57, 59, 60,
    68, 72, 79, 81, 82,
    125, 127, 128, 135, 153,
    169, 180, 194–199, 210,
    235, 249, 307, 310, 312,
    313 *et seq.*, 348, 419,
    520, 536, 698, 705
  Art. 1 .... 82, 127, 313, **749**, 751
    (1)(b) 55
    (c) 65
    (d)(e) 58
    (g) 71
    (k) 67
    (l)(m) 69
    (n) 71
    (o)(p)(q) 750, 752
    2 .... 346, **750**
    3 ....197, 199, 203, **750**
    (1) 201, 314, 752
    (3) 313, 314, 332
    (4) **201**, 203, 314
    4 .... **750**, 751
    5 .... 127, 314, 315, **750**, 751
    6 .... **751**
    7 ....81, **127**, 313, **751**
    (1) 82, 314
    (2) 332
    8 .... **751**, **752**
    (1)(2)(3) 82, 313
    (4) 82
    9 ....197, 314, **752**

Arrest Convention 1952 (Convention relating
  to the Arrest of Sea-Going
  Ships)—*cont.*
  Art. 10 ....201, 750, **752**
  Arts. 11, 12, 13 .... **752**
  Art. 14 .... **752**
    (a) 753
    15 .... **752**
  Arts. 16, 17, 18 .... **753**
Athens Convention 1974 (Convention con-
  cerning the Carriage of Passengers and
  their Luggage by Sea) 15, 79,
    126, 133, 134, 180, 206,
    217, 244, 277, 518, 519
  Art. 2(1) 79, 80
    (2) 79, **80**
    7 519
    17 ....**80**, **133**, 243, 565
    19 79
Brussels Convention 1910 (International Con-
  vention for the Unification of Certain
  Rules of Law with Respect to Collisions
  between Vessels) 127, 402
  Art. 13 751
Brussels Convention 1926 (International Con-
  vention for the Unification of Certain
  Rules relating to the Immunity of State
  Owned Ships) 257, 260
Brussels Convention 1963 126
Brussels Convention 1968 (European Conven-
  tion on Jurisdiction and the Recognition
  and Enforcement of Judgments in Civil
  and Commercial Matters) 4, 15,
    16, 78, 79, 81, 85, 86, 87
    et seq., 101 *et seq.*, 123 *et*
    seq., 159 *et seq.*, 169 *et*
    seq., 179, 180, 182, 185,
    206, 209, 231 *et seq.*, 251,
    264, 269, 276, 283, 295,
    296, 302 *et seq.*, 312 *pas-*
    sim, 351, 354, 382, 383,
    429, 430, 433, 436, 517,
    519, 521, 536, 539, 543,
    547, 549, 565, 595, 607
    passim, 625 *et seq.*, 663 *et*
    seq., **684** *et seq.*, 707, 733

Brussels Convention 1968 (European Conven-
     tion on Jurisdiction and the Recognition
     and Enforcement of Judgments in Civil
     and Commercial Matters)—*cont.*
  Title II 669, 681, 682, 704
          Section 2 ....144, 164
                  3 ....114, 117, 139, 161, 680
                  4 ....117, 139, 161, 164, 680
          Sections 5, 6 164
          III 704
          IV 668
          VII 667
  Arts. 1–20   95
  Art. 1 ....**90**, 105 127, 305,
                                        308, 669, 672–674
       (1) 16, 105, 643
       (2) 163
       2 ....89, 95, **101**, 102, 107, 138,
                              146, 151, 154, **164**, **665**
       3 ....101, 102, 138, **164**, 169, 634, **665**, 667
       a **665**
       b **665**, **666**
       4 ....**101**, 102, 116–118, 124,
                              140, 164, 233, 306, 634
       (2) 102
  Arts. 5–6a   165
  Art. 5 ....88, 137, **144**, **145**, 146, 151, 162
       (1) 89, 97, 108, 109, 115, 117,
                              133, 146–151, 162, 165,
                                        166, 634
       (3) 130, 146, 151, 152, 156, 162, 165
       (4) 154, 155
       (5) 140, 141, 146, 153, 165
       (6) 155, 161, 667
       (7) 135, **152**, **153**
       (8)   165
       5a 164, **166**
       6 ....137, 140, **155**, **156**, 158, 166
       (1) 156, 157, 165, 166
       (2) 114, 156, 157
       (3) 113, 146, 158
       (4)   158
       6a 103, **117**, 134,
                              136, **137**, 155, 166, 536
  Arts. 7–12a   136
  Art. 7 ....117, 140, 141
       8 ....104, 117, 140, 680
       (1)(2)(3)   127
       9   264
       10 ....140, 142, 156
       11 ....140, 141
  Arts. 12–15   167
  Art. 12 ....109, 114, 116, 140, **141** 142–144
       (4) 141, 264
       (5) 141, 142
       12a 116, 140, **141**, 143
       (1)(a)(2)(4)   142
  Arts. 13–15 ....   136, 165
  Art. 13 ..... 104, 117, **143**, **144**, 161, 162, 167, 680
       14 ....117, 161
       (1)   667
       15 ....109, 116, 144, 166, 167

Brussels Convention 1968 (European Conven-
     tion on Jurisdiction and the Recognition
     and Enforcement of Judgments in Civil
     and Commercial Matters)—*cont.*
  Art. 16 ....88, 96, 97, 101, **104**, 105–107, 109,
                      115, 117, 136, 159–161, 163, 164,
                      166, 167, 180, 239, 352, 633, 669
       (1) 158, 264
       (2) ...95, 105, 106, 120, 121, 164, 679, 680
       (3)   106
       (4) 106, 164
       (5) 107, 632
       17 ....98, 104, **108**,
                              109, 110, 112–117, 136,
                              138, 139, 141–144, 147,
                              151, 156, 157, 160, 164,
                              165, **166**, 180, 233, 239
       (2)   638
       18 ....104, **107**, 110, 116, 136,
                              143, 161, 164, 165, 239
       19 ....**97**, 167
       20 ....88, 89, **97**, 98, **99**, 100, 124, 167,
                              608, 634, 637, 638, 651
  Arts. 21–23 ....95, 167, 234, 304
  Art. 21 ....88, 89, 97, 98, **232**,
                              233–238, 307, 608, 630
       22 ....88, 98, **232**, 233–236,
                              238, 239, 537, 630
       23 ....98, 111, **232**, 239
       24 ....95, 180, 233, **303**, 304–308, 310, 628
       25 ....627, 628, 630, 669
       26 ....107, 632, 643, 644
       27 ....626, **635**, 636, 638, 647, 648
       (1) 635, 636
       (2) **100**, 637, **638**, **639**, 640–642, 651
       (3) 99, 233, 236, 642, 643
       (4)   643
       (5) 630, 642, 643
       28 ....626, 633, 635, 638, 647, 648
       29 ....627, 637
       30 ....98, 644, **646**, 647, 648
       31 ....626, 644, **645**, 666
       32 ....645, 666
       33 ....644, 645
       34 ....99, 626, 635, 637, 649
       (3) 627, 637
       35   649
       36 ....649, 650
       37 ....647, 649, 650, 652
       (1)   646
       (2)   666
       38 ....98, 644, 645, **646**, **647**, 648–650
       39 ....310, **649**, 666
       40 ....97–100, 651
       (2)   651
       41 ....651, 652, 666
       43 ....628, 644
       45 ....133, 308, 645
       46 ....645, **646**
       (2)   668
       47 ....645, **646**, 668
       48   646

Brussels Convention 1968 (European Convention on Jurisdiction and the Recognition and Enforcement of Judgments in Civil and Commercial Matters)—*cont.*

Art. 49 646
Arts. 50, 51 626
Art. 52 ....89, 118, 121, 138, 678
  53 ....89, 105, 106, 119, 120, 678, 681
  54 136
  54b(3) 633, 667
Arts. 55–59 630
Art. 55 ....89, 123, 124, 630, 631
  56 ....89, 124, 630
Arts. 57–59 124
Art. 57 .... 89, 101,
      103, 110, 123, **124**, 125, 126,
      128–133, 135–137, 150, 153, 156,
      163, 180, 206, 239, 304, 315, 316,
      536, 625, **630**, 631, 633, 635
  58 ....85, 630
  59 ....89, 102, 630, 633, **634**, 635, 667
Protocol, Art. I 112, **116**, **147**, 634
      II 637
      IV 89, 100, 638
      V **156**, 157
      Vb 97, **146**
      Vd 106
Brussels Convention 1971 (Convention relating to Civil Liability in the Field of Maritime Carriage) 126
CIM Convention 1961 (International Convention concerning Carriage of Goods by Rail)—
Art. 46 217
CIV Convention 1961 (International Convention concerning Carriage of Passengers and Luggage by Rail)—
Art. 46 217
CMR Convention 1956 (Convention on the Contract for the International Carriage of Goods by Road) 79, 80,
      126, 129, 132–134, 217,
      218, 244, 277, 318, 622
Art. 2 ....80, **318**
  (1) 132, 218, 243
  3(1) **318**
  10(2) 80
  14 318
  16 219
  31 .... 132, 133
    (1) 80, **81**, **132**, 631
    (2) **132**, 133
      (a) 133
    (3) 81, 318, **631**
    (4) 318, **631**
    (5) 133
  32 218
  33 277
  36 205
  41 132
COTIF 1980 (International Carriage by Rail Convention) 217

Collision (Civil Jurisdiction) Convention 1952 (International Convention on Certain Rules Concerning Civil Jurisdiction in Matters of Collision) 73, 79, 81, 82, 125,
      126, 128, 129, 135, 156,
      180, 188, 206, 243, 313,
      316, 520, 536
Art. 1 ....**82**, 83, **128**, **754**
  (1)(b) 83
  2 ....**82**, **128**, 533, **754**
  3 ....**82**, **83**, **128**, **754**
  4 .... 82, **754**
ss. 5, 6, 7 .... **754**
s. 8 ....128, **755**
ss. 9, 10, 11, 12, 13, 14 755
  15, 16 .... **756**
Convention of 1869 between the Swiss Confederation and France on Jurisdiction and Enforcement of Judgment in Civil Matters 124, 630, 700, 707
Convention of 1899 between Belgium and France on Jurisdiction and the Validity and Enforcement of Judgments, Arbitration Awards and Authentic Instruments . 699
Convention of 1925 between Belgium and the Netherlands on Jurisdiction, Bankruptcy, and the Validity and Enforcement of Judgments, Arbitration Awards and Authentic Instruments 699
Convention of 1927 for the Execution of Foreign Arbitral Awards 621, 622
Convention of 1929 between the Swiss Confederation and the German Reich on the Recognition and Enforcement of Judgments and Arbitration Awards 707
Convention of 1930 between France and Italy on the Enforcement of Judgments in Civil and Commercial Matters 699
Convention of 1932 between Denmark, Finland, Iceland, Norway and Sweden on the Recognition and Enforcement of Judgments 707
Convention of 1933 on the Recognition and Enforcement of Judgments 707
Convention of 1934 between the United Kingdom and the French Republic providing for the Reciprocal Enforcement of Judgments in Civil and Commercial Matters, with Protocol 699
Convention of 1934 between the United Kingdom and the Kingdom of Belgium providing for the Reciprocal Enforcement of Judgments in Civil and Commercial Matters, with Protocol 699
Convention of 1936 between Germany and Italy on the Recognition and Enforcement of Judgments in Civil and Commercial Matters 699
Convention of 1936 between Sweden and the Swiss Confederation on the Recognition Enforcement of Judgments and Arbitral Awards 707

Convention of 1957 between the Kingdom of Belgium and Austria on the Reciprocal Recognition and Enforcement of Judgments and Authentic Instruments relating to Maintenance Obligations 707

Convention of 1958 between the Federal Republic of Germany and the Kingdom of Belgium on the Mutual Recognition and Enforcement of Judgments, Arbitration Awards and Authentic Instruments in Civil and Commercial Matters 699

Convention of 1959 between the Federal Republic of Germany and Austria on the Reciprocal Recognition and Enforcement of Judgments, Settlements and Authentic Instruments in Civil and Commercial Matters 708

Convention of 1959 between the Kingdom of Belgium and Austria on the Reciprocal Recognition and Enforcement of Judgments, Arbitral Awards and Authentic Instruments in Civil and Commercial Matters 708

Convention of 1959 between the Kingdom of the Netherlands and the Italian Republic on the Recognition and Enforcement of Judgments in Civil and Commercial Matters 699

Convention of 1959 between the Swiss Confederation and Belgium on the Recognition and Enforcement of Judgments and Arbitration Awards 708

Convention of 1960 between Austria and the Swiss Confederation on the Recognition and Enforcement of Judgments 708

Convention of 1960 between the United Kingdom and the Federal Republic of Germany for the Reciprocal Recognition and Enforcement of Judgments in Civil and Commercial Matters 699

Convention of 1961 between Norway and the United Kingdom providing for the Reciprocal Recognition and Enforcement of Judgments in Civil Matters 708

Convention of 1961 between the Kingdom of Greece and the Federal Republic of Germany for the Reciprocal Recognition and Enforcement of Judgments, Settlements and Authentic Instruments in Civil and Commercial Matters 699

Convention of 1962 between the Kingdom of Belgium and the Italian Republic on the Recognition and Enforcement of Judgments and other Enforceable Instruments in Civil and Commercial Matters 699

Convention of 1962 between the Kingdom of the Netherlands and the Federal Republic of Germany on the Mutual Recognition and Enforcement of Judgments and other Enforceable Instruments in Civil and Commercial Matters 699

Convention of 1962 relating to the Liability of Operators of Nuclear Ships 126, 130
    Art. X 130

Convention of 1963 between the Kingdom of the Netherlands and Austria on the Reciprocal Recognition and Enforcement of Judgments and Authentic Instruments in Civil and Commercial Matters 708

Convention of 1966 between France and Austria on the Recognition and Enforcement of Judgments and Authentic Instruments in Civil and Commercial Matters 708

Convention of 1967 between the United Kingdom and the Netherlands providing for the Reciprocal Recognition and Enforcement of Judgments in Civil Matters 699

Convention of 1969 between Spain and France on the Recognition and Enforcement of Judgment Arbitration Awards in Civil and Commercial Matters 699

Convention of 1970 between the United Kingdom and Austria providing for the Reciprocal Recognition and Enforcement of Judgments in Civil and Commercial Matters 708

Convention of 1970 between the United Kingdom and the Republic of Italy for the Reciprocal Recognition and Enforcement of Judgments in Civil and Commercial Matters 699

Convention of 1971 between Italy and Austria on the Recognition and Enforcement of Judgments in Civil and Commercial Matters, of Judicial Settlements and of Authentic Instruments 708

Convention of 1971 between Luxembourg and Austria on the Recognition and Enforcement of Judgments and Authentic Instruments in Civil and Commercial Matters 708

Convention of 1973 between Spain and Italy regarding Legal Aid and the Recognition and Enforcement of Judgments in Civil and Commercial Matters 700

Convention of 1973 on the Grant of European Patents 703

Convention of 1975 for the European Patent for the Common Market—
    Arts. 69(5), 86 703

Convention of 1977 between Denmark, Finland, Iceland, Norway and Sweden on the Recognition and Enforcement of Judgments in Civil Matters 708

Convention of 1977 between Norway and the Federal Republic of Germany on the Recognition and Enforcement of Judgments and Enforceable Documents, in Civil and Commercial Matters 708

Convention of 1982 between Austria and Sweden on the Recognition and Enforcement of Judgments in Civil Matters 708

Convention of 1983 between Spain and the
  Federal Republic of Germany on the Rec-
  ognition and Enforcement of Judgments,
  Settlements and Authentic Instruments in
  Civil and Commercial Matters 700
Convention of 1984 between Austria and
  Spain on the Recognition and Enforce-
  ment of Judgments, Settlements and En-
  forceable Authentic Instruments in Civil
  and Commercial Matters 708
Convention of 1984 between Norway and
  Austria on the Recognition and Enforce-
  ment of Judgments in Civil Matters 708
Convention of 1986 between Finland an Aus-
  tria on the Recognition and Enforcement
  of Judgments in Civil Matters 708
Danube River Navigation Convention 1865 .. 126
Directive 76/308/EEC 183, 732
EFTA Judgments Convention 1988. *See*
  Lugano Convention 1988.
Ems-Dolland bilateral Convention between the
  Netherlands and Germany (Convention
  relating to River Navigation) 125
European Convention on International Com-
  mercial Arbitration 1961 621
European Convention on Jurisdiction and the
  Recognition and Enforcement of Judg-
  ments in Civil and Commercial Matters
  1968. *See* Brussels Convention 1968.
European Convention on State Immunity
  1972 ....257, 258, 620
Funchal Convention 1992 ....561, 581, 714
Fund Convention 1971 (International Conven-
  tion on the Establishment of an Inter-
  national Fund for Compensation for Oil
  Pollution Damage) 35, 53,
                                    54, 81, 84, 126, 129,
                                    130, 219, 522, 540, 632
  Art. 4 130
    (6) 54
    5 130
    7 129
    (3) 130
    8 632
  Protocol 1992 ....30, 53, 54, 84, 126, 129, 540
Fund Convention 1992 (International Conven-
  tion on the Establishment of an Inter-
  national Fund for Compensation for Oil
  Pollution Damage) 540, 632
Geneva Convention 1927 (Convention on the
  Execution of Foreign Arbitral Awards) .. 275
Geneva Protocol 1923 on Arbitration
  Clauses 275
Hague Convention 1964 (Convention relating
  to the Uniform Law on the International
  Sale of Goods)—
  Art. 59 150

Hague Convention 1965 (Convention on the
  Service Abroad of Judicial and Extra
  Judicial Documents in Civil or Commer-
  cial Matters) ...89, 186, 187, 628, 637, 639, 734
  Arts. 1, 10 638
  Art. 15 ....**99,** 123, 638, 691
    19 638
Hague Convention 1970 (Convention on the
  Taking of Evidence Abroad in Civil or
  Commercial Matters) 628
Hague Rules 1924 ....78, 126, 131,
                                    214, 243, 244, 519
  Art. 3(8) **131**
    8 131
Hague-Visby Rules 1968 ....78, 79, 81, 126,
                      131, 213–215, 217, 218, 220, 225,
                      228, 243, 244, 288, 317, 519, 534,
                                                563, 565
  Art. III, r. 6 .... **219**
    r. 8 ....**131,** 244, 245, 577
    VI 518
    VIII 131, **245,** 519
    IX **131**
    X **563**
Hamburg Rules 1978 .... 15, 78, 84, 126, 131,
                      132, 313, 316, 318, 519, 585
  Art. 2(1) **131**
    5 518
    17 277
    21 ....205, 243, 317, 565
    (1) 131, **316**
    (2) 131, **317**
    (3)(4) 132
    (5) 132, **317**
    22 ....131, 277, 317
    (4)(5) 277
    25(2) 317, 318
    (5) 318
International Regulations for Preventing Colli-
  sions at Sea 1972 ....563, 593, 594
  reg. 2 593
Inter-American Convention on International
  Commercial Arbitration 1975 621
International Convention on Tonnage Meas-
  urements of Ships 1969—
  Art. 6(5) 522
Liability Convention 1969. *See* Oil Pollution
  Convention 1969.
Limitation Convention 1924 (International
  Convention for the Unification of Certain
  Rules relating to the Limitation of Liabi-
  lity of Owners of Sea Going Ships) 319, 518
Limitation Convention 1957 (International
  Convention relating to the Limitation of
  Liability of Owners of Sea Going
  Ships) 319, 339, 421, 518, 519, 521,
                                    522, 525, 528, 529, 531, 534

Limitation Convention 1976 (Convention on
  the Limitation of Liability for Maritime
  Claims) 126, 134, 135, 137, 239, 244, 253,
           254, 260, 313, 319, 325, 339, 340,
           345, 414, 509, 517 *passim*, 572
  Art. 1 .... 522, 524
    (7) 522
    2 524
    (1) **524**
    (2) **525**
    3 ....263, 524, 525
    (e) 528
    4 .... 524, 525
    6 .... 525, 526
    (3) 526
  Arts. 7, 8(2) 526
  Art. 9 522
    10 523
  Arts. 11–14 526
  Art. 11 ....134, 339, 523, 738
    12(1) 519
    (3) 538
    13 .... **134**
    (1) 522, 527
    (2) 319, **339**, 522, 527
    (3) 319
    14 ....526, 538, 562
    15 523
    (4) 522, 523
    (5) 522
    18(1) 523, 524
Lugano Convention 1988 (EFTA Judgments
  Convention). *See also* Brussels Conven-
  tion 1968 .... 16, 79, 85, 86, 123,
         159, 161, 169 *et seq.*, 179, 185,
         206, 209, 231 *et seq.*, 264, 269,
         276, 283, 295, 296, 302 *et seq.*,
         312 *passim*, 351, 354, 382, 383,
         429, 430, 433, 436, 517, 519, 521,
         536, 539, 543, 565, 607 *passim*,
         625 *et seq.*, 664 *et seq.*, **704**, 733
  Title II 161, 704
    Section 2 704
    Sections 3, 4 680
    Section 5 704
  Title IV 668
    VII 667
  Art. 3 169
    5(1) 170
    16 .... 170, 352
    (1) 169
    17 .... 169, 170
    28 635
    54A 169
    54B 170, 667
    57(4) 635
    61 664
  Protocol No. 2 665
Luxembourg Convention 1984 (Convention on
  the Accession of the Hellenic Republic to
  the Rome Convention) 561, 581, 714, **723**

Mannheim Convention 1868. *See* Rhine Nav-
  igation Convention 1868.
Maritime Liens and Mortgages Convention
  1926 (Convention for the Unification of
  Certain Rules Relating to Maritime Liens
  and Mortgages) 25, 69, 71, 126,
         135, 153, 312, 313, 319,
         374, 410, 418, 419, 511,
         519, 632
  Art. 1 419
    2 .... 419, 420
  Arts. 3, 4, 5 420
  Art. 7 ....418, 420, 519
  Arts. 8, 9, 10, 11, 13 420
  Art. 14 418
    15 ....418, 419
Maritime Liens and Mortgages Convention
  1967 (Convention for the Unification of
  Certain Rules Relating to Maritime Liens
  and Mortgages) 25, 69, 71, 126, 135,
         153, 312, 313, 319, 374, 410,
         418–420, 423, 425, 511, 519, 632
  Arts. 1, 2, 3, 4, 5 421
  Art. 6 .... 422, 439
  Arts. 7, 8, 10 421
  Art. 11 632
    (1)(2) 422
    12 418
    (2) 421
    14 418
    (2) 519
    19 420
Maritime Liens and Mortgages Convention
  1993 (International Convention on Mar-
  itime Liens and Mortgages) 25, 69,
         126, 135, 153, 312, 313, 319, 374,
         410, 418, 419, 422, 511, 519, 632
  Arts. 1–3 423
  Art. 1 ....**756, 757**, 758
    2 .... **757**
    3 ....423, **757**, 760
    4 ....423, **757**, 758–760
    5 ....423, 424, **758**
    6 .... 425, **758**
    7 ....424, 439, **758**
    8 .... 424, **758**
    9 ....226, 424, **758**, 759
    10 ....424, 758, **759**
    11 .... 424, 757, **759**, 760, 761
    12 ....424, 425, 632, 757, 758, **759**, **760**
    (1) 423
    (3) 758
    (4) 424, 758
    (5) 757, 761
    13 ....423, **760**
    (1)(2) 418
    14 760
    15 ....418, 419, 519, **760**
    16 ....423, **760**, **761**
    17 .... **761**
    18 ....418, **761**
  Arts. 19, 20 .... **761**

Maritime Liens and Mortgages Convention 1993 (International Convention on Maritime Liens and Mortgages)—*cont.*
Arts. 21, 22 .... **762**
Moselle River Navigation Convention 1956 (Luxembourg, Germany and France) 126
Multimodal Convention 1980 .... 126, 132
Art. 26 .... 132, 243
Arts. 27, 30 132
New York Convention on the Recognition and Enforcement of Foreign Arbitral Awards 1958 .... 92, 273, 274, 276, 280, 281, 621–623, 656, 659
Art. I(3) 274
Arts. IV, V, VII 275
Oil Pollution Convention 1969 (Convention on Civil Liability for Oil Pollution Damage) ... 53, 54, 83, 126, 129, 130, 219, 261, 518, 522, 525, 540, 632
Arts. II, V 129
Art. IX **129**, 130, 632
(1) **83**
X **632**
Protocol 1992 .... 30, 53, 83, 126, 129, 540
Oil Pollution Damage Convention 1992 (International Convention on Civil Liability for Oil Pollution Damage) 81, 83, 540, 632
Paris Convention 1960 (Convention on Third Party Liability in the Field of Nuclear Energy) 126, 130
Art. 13 .... 130, 632
Paris Convention 1963 (Convention on Third Party Liability in the Field of Nuclear Energy) 84, 130
Protocol of 1923 on Arbitral Clauses 621
Protocol of 1964 relating to the Paris Conventions of Third Party Liability in the Field of Nuclear Energy 126, 130
Protocol of 1971 (Luxembourg, 3 June 1971) 88, 149, 305, 663, 665, 672, 683, 704, 707
Arts. 2, 4, 37 88
Protocol of 1977 relating to the Treaty on Merchant Navigation 327
Protocol of 1988 (First Brussels Protocol on the Interpretation of the Rome Convention by the European Court) 169, 561, 582, 714, 715, **724–727**
Rhine Navigation Convention 1868 .... 81, 84, 126, 127, 135, 136, 264, 654, 662, 663, 751, 754
Art. 34 .... **135, 265**
34II(c) 135, 136
35 .... 135, 136
(b) 135, **136**
(c) **136**
Rome Convention 1980 (Convention on the Law Applicable to Contractual Obligations) .... 148, 215, 240, 277, 561, 565, 574, 579, 581, 596, 597, 604, 714 *et seq.*, **716** *et seq.*

Rome Convention 1980 (Convention on the Law Applicable to Contractual Obligations)—*cont.*
Art. 1 .... **582**
(3) 714
2 .... 574, 582
3 .... 583, 585, 586
(3) 585
4 .... 583, 586
(1) 586
(2) 586–588
(3)(4) 586
(5) 586–588
5 582
(1)(2)(3)(4)(5) 582
6(1)(2) 582
7(1) 585, 714
(2) 585
8 .... 576, 584
(1)(2) 566
9 576
(1)(4)(5)(6) 584
10(1)(e) 714
11 .... 576, 582, 583
12 .... 571, 584
(2) 599
13 599
(1)(2) 584
14 .... 582, 583
15 576
16 .... 562, 570, 585
19(2) 714
22(3) 715
Salvage Convention 1989 .... 26, 28, 31, 64, 214, 244, 262, 326, 654, 655, 660
Art. 1 .... 473, 598
(6) 395, 399
3 .... 27, 395
7 596
15 410
(2) 598
16 .... 30, 502
20 .... 27, 30, 395, 397, 399, 418
(1) 417
(2) 417, 419
23 .... 219, **222**
San Sebastian Convention 1989—
Art. 25(2)(b) 630
Treaty of Rome 87, 309, 626
Art. 7 133
177 88
188 726
220 .... 685, 701
Rules of Procedure of the European Court of Justice 726
Treaty of 1896 between the Swiss Confederation and Spain on the Mutual Enforcement of Judgments in Civil and Commercial Matters 707

Maritime Claims and their Consequences

1. THE TRIPARTITE NATURE OF MARITIME CLAIMS

Of what legal consequence is it that a claim is "maritime" in nature—or, to put it another way "lies in Admiralty"? This book deals with the jurisdictional, remedial and security consequences which follow simply from the inclusion of a claim within Admiralty jurisdiction. Naturally, in any legal system, any particular consequences are built on and into the framework of that system as a whole. It is, therefore, essential to consider not only the rules applicable to Admiralty as such but those governing claims generally and applied to maritime as any other claims. Note must thereby be carefully taken of domestic differences between Admiralty and other claims.

There are three enforcement aspects of maritime claims:

   (i) the extent to which "security" may be obtained by a maritime claimant so as to ensure that there will be assets available to turn a judgment into material gain (*the provisional remedy aspect*);

  (ii) the rules governing the bringing of an action to enforce a maritime claim (*the jurisdictional aspect*);

 (iii) the extent to which a maritime claimant becomes a preferred creditor (*the security aspect*).

In many legal systems based on codes this logical (and indeed chronological) order is borne out in legislation. Rules of provisional remedy will be found in the Civil Procedure Code, unless there are particular maritime rules which may then be included in the Maritime Code. Rules relating to jurisdiction on the merits will probably be found similarly in procedure codes but distinguished from rules relating to provisional remedy. Rules relevant to preferred creditors will be in the Maritime Code, in so far as these are maritime rules and in the Civil Code in so far as they are generally applicable.

In English law we are not blessed with such logic. The rules are to be found partly in legislative act—statute or procedural rule of court—and partly in judicial statements in decided cases. The three aspects of provisional remedy, jurisdiction on the merits and preferred claims are inextricably intermingled, and terminology is heavy with confusion between the three, in particular because of the use of "lien".

THE CONCEPT OF "LIEN"—AND ITS CONNECTION WITH ARREST AND JURISDICTION

In common legal parlance a lien is a security concept indicating that the claim protected by it can be asserted against the asset in which the lien is held. It indicates a right enforceable against purchasers and, to some extent, a preferred claim enforceable in priority to unsecured creditors. In English law it developed from the "possessory lien" which provides only a passive right of retention of an asset in support of a claim. While such a lien remains of importance, other liens providing for more aggressive assertion of claims are now also established. In particular, since 1851 English law has recognized the concept of the "maritime lien".

The concept of the lien fits well with maritime claims, for historically in English law such claims traditionally attracted the ability to enforce them, at least to some extent, against particular assets. Provided the appropriate procedure is followed, this ability makes the maritime claimant a preferred creditor. It is an easy step, therefore, not to restrict the term to claims attracting a "maritime lien" but to label each "preferred" maritime claim a 'lien'. Further, as the appropriate procedure is to issue a writ commencing an action on the merits (a writ *in rem*), the idea of lien is linked to the availability of a particular kind of action on a maritime claim (i.e. jurisdiction *in rem*); and as that kind of action (action *in rem*) carried with it a provisional remedy (arrest) so that aspect became connected to jurisdiction and security.

A final terminological step is to use "lien" to describe the whole—(i.e. the claim having remedial, jurisdictional and security aspects)—and thereby to conceal the differing aspects of the parts. The reasons for the intermingling of the jurisdictional, remedial and security parts into this somewhat misleading whole are historical. The time has surely come for a determined attempt to separate what are quite distinct matters of policy. Failure to do so has played its part in ratification of at least one international Convention without compliance domestically with its provisions, a surprising inability to adapt fully the availability of the most effective provisional remedy (arrest) to arbitration, in uncertainty as to the security effect of actions available to maritime claimants and priority as between maritime claims.

2. THE RELEVANCE OF A FOREIGN ELEMENT

A maritime claim is more likely than not to be connected with more than one State. By the nature of maritime activity it is highly probable that not all events relevant to a claim will have occurred in the State in which it is sought to enforce that claim. It follows that any attempt to pursue such a claim in any State will probably raise a preliminary question of jurisdiction in the courts of that State. Certainly this may be so for any claim with a foreign element which is brought in England.

Relevant to the hearing of a claim in any court and the parties' interest in which court is first the availability of interim relief in relation to the action. Also material is the law which will govern the substantive issues, the ability to enforce the judgment against the defendant's assets in the State where proceedings are brought or elsewhere and whether lacking such enforcement the bringing of proceedings affects the ability to start again in the same or another State.

In turn relevant to these matters is the extent to which any national law will recognize that a party has a choice or even an opportunity to make representations as to jurisdiction. Further, the question of recognition or enforcement of a judgment in a State other than that in which it was obtained may arise independently of that of jurisdiction to hear the case. In that event a plaintiff will simply be anxious to enforce a claim through the judgment without the necessity of starting new proceedings.

3. STATUTORY AND CONVENTION DEVELOPMENT

Statutes

The development reflects a (sometimes ill-fitting) joining of history and international agreements.

Until 1956

Since the nineteenth century, domestic Admiralty jurisdiction has depended partly on the building up of a framework by the judiciary and partly on statute. Modern jurisdiction is rooted in the Admiralty Court Acts 1840 and 1861 and the codified extension of the Supreme Court of Judicature (Consolidation) Act 1925. One of the major problems of construction was to assess the effect of the statutory extension of Admiralty jurisdiction on the concepts developed prior to 1840—and in particular the relationship of Admiralty jurisdiction to the attachment of liens to maritime claims, traditionally a hallmark of Admiralty.

The Administration of Justice Act 1956

In 1956 the grounds of claim within Admiralty jurisdiction were again codified and extended in the Administration of Justice Act, but even here history took its toll. The statute of 1956 reflected the international approach in taking as its primary base the Convention Relating to the Arrest of Sea Going Ships 1952 (hereafter the Arrest Convention). It was, however, not bold enough—or internationally minded enough—to make a break with history. First the statute (unlike the Convention) made no attempt to distinguish between "arrest" and jurisdiction over the hearing of a claim on the merits. Secondly, the statute persisted in using the "maritime lien" as a jurisdictional ground while failing to define the nature or content of the concept. Thirdly, in addition to the Convention claims it included a catch-all provision incorporating claims historically recognized as part of English Admiralty.

An opportunity to set out effectively Admiralty jurisdiction, provisional remedies and security aspects and to bring closer together the common and civil law approach was missed in 1956. Instead a major fundamental defect was written even more distinctively and directly into the English maritime legal framework. The grounds of claim were specified, the type of action (in personam or in rem) to enforce them was specified to some extent, but the provisional remedy and security aspects ignored.

The Supreme Court Act 1981

In 1981 came another chance to introduce a comprehensive code with the replacement of the relevant provisions of the Administration of Justice Act 1956 by provisions of the Supreme Court Act 1981. A major change was proposed to bring English law into line with the Arrest Convention. But shipowners and their insurers awaking (actually or tactically) a little late to the effect that compliance with international obligations would have on them persuaded the Government to think again. While it was thinking again it could well have thought about codifying those parts of Admiralty jurisdiction, provisional remedy and security that statutes as yet do not reach.

Conventions enacted into English law

A number of Conventions enacted into English law contain jurisdiction provisions relating to maritime claims. In this way specific jurisdiction prerequisites are introduced in respect of particular claims. Further, the framework of maritime claims in general is, as has been said, intended to reflect the Arrest Convention.

Civil Jurisdiction and Judgments Acts 1982 and 1991

The most far reaching and radical changes to English Admiralty jurisdiction were encompassed in the general shift of the jurisdiction for commercial claims from procedure to a substantive link following United Kingdom membership of the European Community. The changes are reflected in the jurisdiction and judgments structure set out in the Convention on Jurisdiction and the Recognition and Enforcement of Judgments in Civil and Commercial Matters agreed by the original member States in 1968 and amended on the accession of each new State. A "parallel" Convention 1988 creates an almost identical structure in respect of States members of the European Union and the European Free Trade Association.

As a consequence of the 1982 and 1991 Acts there is one jurisdiction and judgment structure for cases connected with Europe and another (national) for other cases. The complexity increases, underlining the need for an Admiralty Code in English law. Any further codification or recodification of the Merchant Shipping Acts should not exclude those parts of "shipping law" going to jurisdiction and procedure.

The codification of the Merchant Shipping Act 1995 regrettably does not encompass those parts of "shipping law" pertaining to jurisdiction and procedure save those that appeared in a piecemeal way in earlier statutes dealing with substantive matters. Such are the substantive consequences of the action *in rem* and the uncertainties of liens that any "codification" without them is partial only.

4. MATCHING STATUTE AND CONVENTION

The need for a statutory clear and updated statement of all aspects of maritime claims has been emphasized by the continued reliance on historical Admiralty practice to interpret the current statutory framework. In 1967 in *The Monica S*[1] counsel argued that the

---

1. [1968] P. 741.

Administration of Justice Act 1956 was merely declaratory of pre-existing law in that an action *in rem* became effective on arrest of a ship and not issue of a writ *in rem*. This argument was rejected by Brandon J. both on the authorities and on the basis that, if prior to 1956, the rule had been as argued the question should be decided by "the ordinary and natural construction" to be put on the statute. And that led also to the rejection of the argument. But the very fact that the statute is so worded as to allow the argument to be raised is a defect in the approach to a modern Admiralty framework.

In 1981 in *Tehno-Impex* v. *Gebr. van Weelde Scheepvaartkantoor B.V.*[2] Oliver L.J. took a restricted view of the power of maritime arbitrators to award interest by way of damages for late payment. He held the power to be limited to interest on claims falling within the jurisdiction of the Admiralty Court under the Admiralty Court Act 1861. The extension of Admiralty Court jurisdiction (as then reflected in the Administration of Justice Act 1956) did not mean that the civil rules applicable to the old jurisdiction outside Admiralty applied to the new extension to Admiralty. He thought it would be extraordinary that an Act passed to comply with obligations under the Arrest Convention had by a side-wind freed one division of the High Court from a restrictive rule while leaving the rule untouched in other divisions.

Fortunately, it may be said, Oliver L.J. was in the minority. To follow his rationale is still to require constant reference back to the date on which the Admiralty Court acquired jurisdiction over a particular kind of claim. Further examples of an unduly restrictive, because historical, approach are decisions of the House of Lords in *The Goring*[3]—geographical scope of a salvage action—and *The River Rima*[4]—the supply of goods to a ship. In the latter the House of Lords even construed the Convention Relating to the Arrest of Sea Going Ships in the light of English law prior to the Convention (see Chapter 2).

However the judicial trend over the last 10 years has not always been backward. First, the courts have shown themselves more ready to accept that the United Kingdom is part of the European Community than have many politicians. Secondly, there have been a number of decisions accepting consequential legal changes from radical statutory development.[5] The legislative pattern must bear part of the responsibility for any reluctance to move forward—for failing to develop and put the *whole* framework into statutory form. This failure is heightened by attempting to comply with a Convention on Arrest through the introduction of statutes focused on actions on the merits. English law traditionally *made* not only the availability of "security" for a claim but provisional remedy depend on jurisdiction over the claim on the merits. It is, therefore, actions on the merits which must be considered first in any analysis of the Admiralty framework—even though there are now distinct signs of recognition that there is not necessarily an equation in jurisdiction terms between merits and ancillary orders.

2. [1981] 1 Q.B. 648. In *The La Pintada* [1984] 2 Lloyd's Rep. 9 the House of Lords overruled *Tehno-Impex*—but the point made in the text as to constant reference back remains.
3. [1988] A.C. 831; [1988] 1 Lloyd's Rep. 397.
4. [1988] 2 Lloyd's Rep. 193 (H.L.).
5. See e.g. *The Bazias 3 and 4* [1993] 1 Lloyd's Rep. 101 (as to which see Chap. 15; *The Capitan San Luis* [1993] 2 Lloyd's Rep. 573, as to which see Chap. 24.